The PC NOVICE'S Handbook

Harshad Kotecha

Second Edition November 1992

Computer Step
Warwick CV34 6LP
England

Notice of Liability:
Every effort has been made to ensure that this book contains accurate and current information. However, Computer Step and the author shall not be liable for any loss or damage suffered by readers as a result of any information contained herein.

Trademarks:
All trademarks are acknowledged as belonging to their respective companies.

Printed in England

ISBN 1 874029 04 0

This book is dedicated to all PC Novices that helped to produce it - with their contributions on the value of its contents to them personally. Their comments and suggestions have helped to produce this invaluable guide for all computer novices.

About the Author

Harshad Kotecha graduated in Computer Studies in 1983. Since then, he has worked in the computer industry at various levels. His work has included presenting the benefits of using particular computer systems in large organisations and providing training to individuals. He has also written several other computer books and manuals.

In this book he is using his extensive experience to provide a comprehensive guide for beginners: to buy the right personal computer, to get started and to learn more.

Preface

Just over a decade ago we saw the birth of the IBM PC. In this relatively short time, the PC has increased in power and complexity beyond anyone's wildest dreams. It is estimated that there are now over 150 million personal computer users worldwide, and that this number is growing rapidly. Despite this phenomenal growth, there are still many people who feel alienated by computers.

Hence, we have the modern paradox of a computer age in which substantial numbers of individuals are detached from the benefits of owning and using a computer.

The purpose of this book is to redress this imbalance in a concise, jargon-free language. You will not need a computer dictionary to understand this book. You don't even need a PC initially. In fact, you'll be able to make a wiser purchasing decision about which PC and software to buy once you have read this book.

This book will also enable you to competently talk to computer dealers and colleagues at work. And you'll be able to understand and follow the growing number of computer publications.

More specifically, areas covered in this book are:

1. The PC Unravelled

Expains the various components of a PC, including items commonly used with a PC, like printers. Describes options available as well as the benefits.

2. Software Solutions

The benefits of all major types of business software is explained here. You will also learn about the important features to look for in software packages.

3. Let's Go Shopping

The author takes you shopping with him if you have not already bought a system. Different sources for choosing, and the criteria to use when buying your system are described. Also, interesting tips and advice is offered if you are not familiar with the computer jungle.

4. DOS and all that Jazz

Once you have a system, DOS will enable you to take greater advantage of it. This is not a difficult language, but essential if you want to use your PC seriously. Also, learn how *Windows* can open many more doors for you.

5. Let your PCs do the talking

After you have mastered your own PC, you may want it to communicate with other computers. Computer Communications is usually a very technical topic. The essential basics described here are the most comprehensible you will find anywhere.

6. The Last Word

Finally, find out how you can further your knowledge after you have read this book.

Conventions used

Commands that you can type on your PC and messages displayed by the PC are in this typeface:

```
This is the computer typeface
```

Whenever you are required to press the Enter key (also known as the Return key), usually after typing a command, it is denoted by:

↵

Table of Contents

The PC Unravelled

Computers fall into three main categories: mainframes, mini-computers (sometimes called *minis*) and micro-computers (*micros*). Mainframes and mini-computers are usually used by large organisations. They can process a lot more information and tend to be more complex. These computers were in use well before the first micro was built and are beyond the scope of this book.

Micros, or micro-computers were labelled as such because when they were first built they were not taken seriously - they were thought to be too small to be serious computers. In fact, the early micro-computers were games machines built by computer hobbyists in their garages.

A PC is the most popular family of micro-computers today. PC stands for Personal Computer. Because of its size and price it can be purchased to meet just one person's computing needs. Since 1981, when IBM introduced its own micro-computer, called IBM-PC, the term PC has been used to refer to the IBM PC and all other computers with similar specification. These IBM clones are commonly known as 'IBM PC compatibles'.

An IBM PC compatible machine must be able to run the same programs as the IBM PC. For example, Lotus 1-2-3 (a well known program for the PC) must work in the same way on the compatible as it will on the IBM PC. Also, peripherals like the printer, must be interchangeable with the IBM PC.

A PC in a modern office

Hardware

Your computer consists of hardware and software. Hardware is the term used to refer to the physical, tangible elements of your computer. These are parts you can see and touch. Software (or programs), on the other hand consists of encoded statements, which instruct the computer to perform the required tasks. A floppy disk you insert in your PC, for instance, is hardware. The programs on it are collectively termed software. Software is an important part of your computer. Without it your computer is simply a mass of electronic components.

The subject of software deserves a whole chapter of its own. The next chapter is dedicated to cover this topic in detail. The rest of this chapter looks at PC hardware.

A PC consists of the following basic hardware parts:

- Keyboard
- Monitor
- System Unit

Keyboard

The keyboard is an essential input device that you need to give instructions to your computer. The keys are essentially the same as those found on a typewriter. A computer keyboard, however, will have some additional keys:

Enter ↵

When you type commands from your keyboard, you need to press the Enter key. It is only when you press this key that the computer reads your entry. This key is also used like the 'carriage return' on a typewriter to mark the end of a paragraph.

Control (marked 'Ctrl') and Alternative ('Alt')

These are used with each other or other keys for specific purposes, largely dictated by software. For instance, 'Ctrl', 'Alt', and 'Delete' keys are pressed together to restart, or in computer terminology, reboot your PC.

Function keys

These are labelled F1, F2, F3 and so on until F12. They are used by various software packages to instruct the PC to perform specific tasks. For example, F1 will usually provide instant on-screen help on your software.

Escape (marked Esc)

Again largely controlled by software. It is usually used to go back from a specific screen or option selected from a software application.

Page Up, Page Down, Insert & Delete

These keys are usually used within a word processor. They allow you to page up and down in a long document or edit text using Insert or Delete keys.

Arrow keys

There are four keys near the numeric key-pad on the right; each with an arrow pointing in different directions. These enable you to move the cursor (dash or a square block on the screen used for positioning) around the screen.

Print Screen

Allows you to print an image of your screen onto paper.

Although you will hear people say that IBM keyboards are the best, a lot depends on your own preferences. IBM keyboards have a 'positive feel' which means that they click when you press a key. Some keyboards such as Compaqs' are silent. The best way to choose a keyboard is to try typing on a few. Buy the one that feels right.

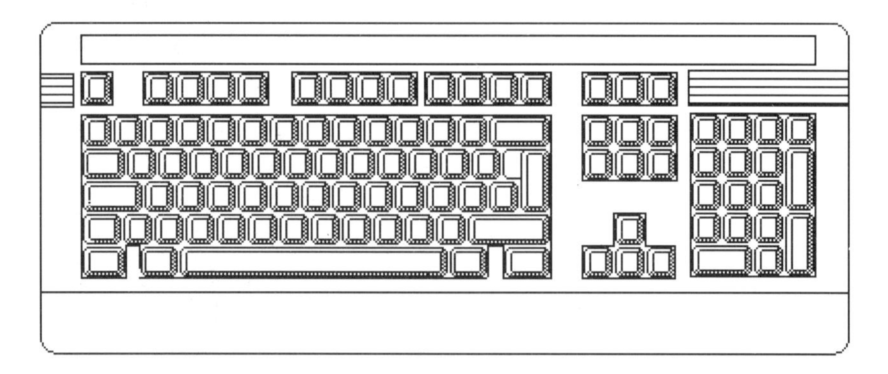

Standard PC Keyboard

Note that the layout of keys may vary slightly on your particular keyboard.

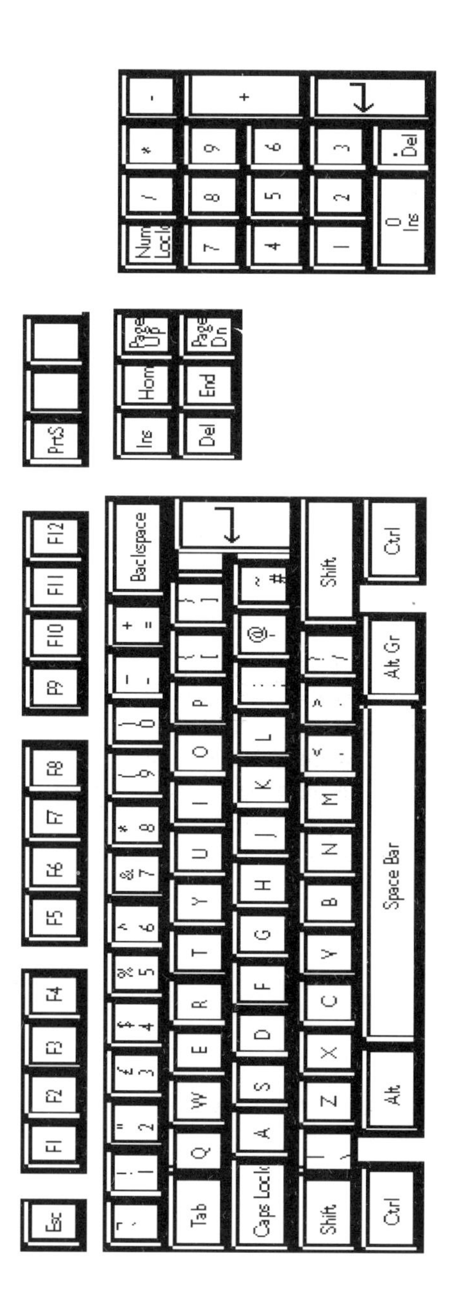

Keyboard layout

Monitor

The monitor is necessary for you to see what you are typing. Your computer needs it to tell you what is going on and to show you the results of the tasks you have asked it to perform. If the keyboard is the main device for you to talk to your computer, then the monitor is the main device for your computer to talk to you.

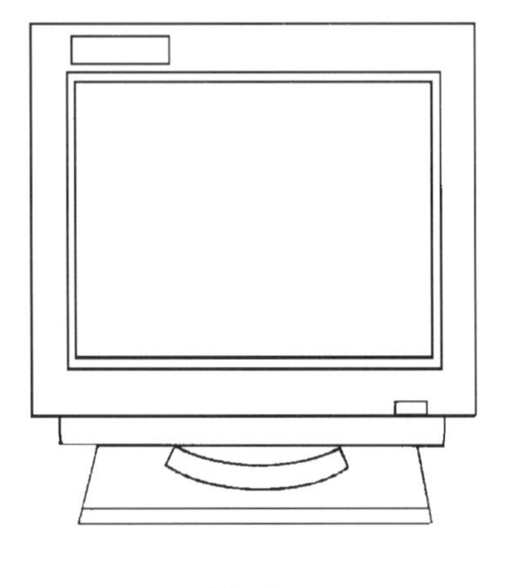

Monitor

Monitors are also called screens, video display units (VDUs) or just displays. Monitors look just like your portable television sets. In fact, earlier home computers did not come with monitors. Television screens were used instead. This is a cheaper alternative but the display quality is poor compared to the dedicated monitors you can buy as part of your computer.

Today the choice of monitors available is extensive. However, you only need to be aware of major distinctions between the various types.

A PC monitor is controlled by an 'expansion card' (circuit board) that is placed inside the computer before the monitor is installed. This card is known as 'video/graphics adapter'. An expansion card translates data from the computer into signals that can be understood by the monitor. The monitor and the expansion card must be compatible with each other for this to work. There are two types of cards: monochrome and colour. Within the two, there are several choices:

Monochrome

Monochrome screen displays in one colour. Monochrome screens are usually cheaper than colour ones. They are also sometimes better for reading text. The letters and numbers are displayed much more clearly.

The most basic (and the earliest) cards available for monochrome screens are *Monochrome Display Adapters* (MDA). These work perfectly with text but do not support graphics.

A company called Hercules Computers in USA came up with a better method in 1982. It introduced the *Hercules Graphics Adapter* (HGA), which supported graphics as well as text. Hercules graphics card became the industry standard and today you will see many other companies offering graphics adapters that are 'Hercules-Compatible'. While the screens are monochrome, these cards enable you to produce graphics by a range of tones of the same colour.

Colour

Colour monitors are better suited for graphical applications (including games). These monitors cost more than monochromes but they do offer more interesting displays. The choice of colour screens is even wider. Again the screen type is identified by the video adapter inside the PC.

The basic and the cheapest colour screen is called the CGA screen. CGA stands for *Colour Graphics Adapter*. Although a lot of software has been developed to support CGA, due to its popularity in early days, you will not be overjoyed with the display. For text processing, CGA screens are quite a strain on the eyes when used continuously. As for graphics, a CGA screen can only display four colours at a time.

Next comes the EGA *(Enhanced Graphics Adapter)* screens. These give a much better resolution than the CGA and can display sixteen colours. Although expensive in the early days, they have fallen in price and are now very affordable.

Most of the EGA screens are also Hercules-compatible.

The most popular colour screens today must be the ones with VGA cards. IBM introduced this standard when it introduced the PS/2 series of computers in 1988. The technology underlying these screens is quite different from the earlier colour cards. Hence its name, *Video Graphics Array* (VGA). VGA screens offer even better resolution than EGA.

The latest screens to be introduced in the market are all based on the same technology as VGA. These are:

- Super VGA
- EVGA (Extended VGA)
- VGA Plus

These are more expensive than the ones discussed above but offer high resolution and can display many colours.

System Unit

The system unit is the primary part of your PC. It is a plastic or a metal case containing several important elements that makes a computer what it is.

The basic parts that reside within the system unit are:

- Microprocessor
- Memory
- Hard Disk
- Floppy Disk Drive

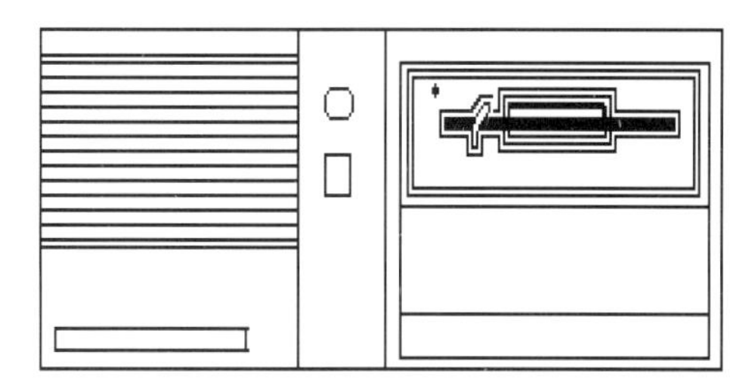

The System Unit

Microprocessor

A microprocessor is often referred to as the 'brain' of a computer. This is because it is here that all the work is done. The processor (also called CPU - Central processing Unit) obeys software instructions and manipulates relevant data. It has the ultimate control over all other components, such as the memory, hard disk and printer.

A microprocessor is a microchip, similar to those found in washing machines, microwaves and television sets. Most PC manufacturers use microchips produced by Intel Corporation, with names such as 8086 and 80286. These chips determine the PC's character. For example, a PC with a 80286 chip will work much faster than a PC with 8086. The names given to PCs are based on the type of chip it contains. The name usually includes a reference to the chip used in the PC. E.g. Amstrad's PC 3386SX. The higher the chip number, the more powerful the computer, and of course the price tag is higher too.

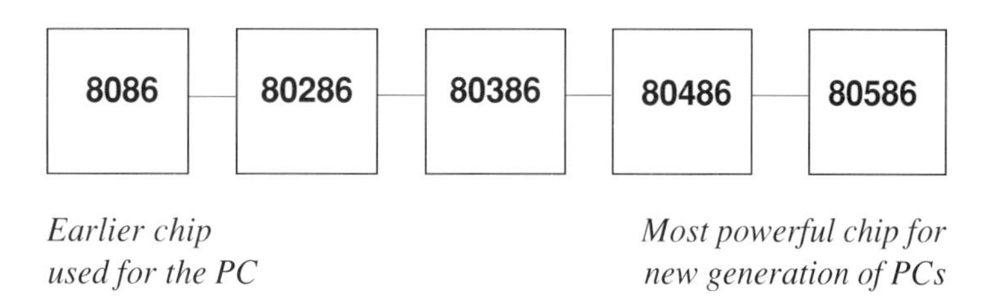

Memory

Computer memory holds information that is required by the processor. This information may be the data to be processed or the programs to process the data. On the surface, the memory is just another microchip. However, what is crucial is what the chip contains. There are two types of memory: *Read Only Memory* (ROM) and *Random Access Memory* (RAM).

Read Only Memory

When you switch on your PC you will notice that it takes a few seconds before it allows you to enter any commands. During these few seconds the PC is running various routines. These routines, or programs, consist of self tests for the PC to ensure that all its parts are working properly. These programs are held in the ROM. The other software that resides within the ROM are programs to take care of routine jobs such as reading instructions from the keyboard and sending characters to the screen. Everything in the ROM has to be installed when the chip is manufactured and you cannot change or erase its contents. Hence, it is called Read Only Memory.

Random Access Memory

When you switch on your PC, RAM is available to store information. Unlike the data held in ROM, the data in RAM can be changed or erased. However, RAM just holds 'live' data consisting of the software you are using plus any data files that you may create or update. When you switch off your PC everything in RAM is wiped off.

The size of your RAM is quite important. You must have enough RAM to hold your software and data. If you are going to be using your PC for large, complex applications, then you will need enough RAM for them. All software requires a certain amount of RAM. This is one of the main reasons why you should decide on which software you are going to use, before you buy the hardware. This issue is discussed in more detail later.

Although it is possible to add more RAM to your PC later, you will save yourself much hassle (and money) by buying enough in the first instance.

Hard Disk

RAM is a temporary storage media. For more permanent storage you need to use disks. These may be floppy disks or hard disks. They both work in the same way as your cassette tapes. Disks are coated with a magnetic film on which data is written. Hard disks, however, are made to be more robust with aluminium casing rather than the plastic casing used for floppies. Hard disks can also store a lot more data. The other benefit of having a hard disk is that the processor can access data from a hard disk 10 times faster than from a floppy disk. Hence, the PC can work much faster. If you are going to use your PC for serious applications, then you should definitely have a hard disk.

Hard Disk shown with read/write head

Nowadays, hard disks are usually part of your PC and sit within the system unit. The storage capacity of hard disks typically starts at 20 megabytes and can run into hundreds of megabytes. A megabyte (Mb for short) is just over a million characters. So a 20 Mb hard disk can store over twenty million characters.

Even if you have a hard disk, you will still need a disk drive to read floppy disks. When you buy software it will come on one or more floppy disks. These floppies are used to install the software onto the hard disk, where it is stored until required. Everytime you use the software, it is transferred to the RAM automatically. The processor then addresses this memory to process instructions and data stored here.

Floppy Disk Drive

The disk drive size and the floppy disk sizes must be compatible. In the PC world, floppy disks come in two sizes: 5¼" and 3½". These are the diameters of the disks. Your disk drive, which looks like a hole on the face of your system unit, will be able to read one or the other:

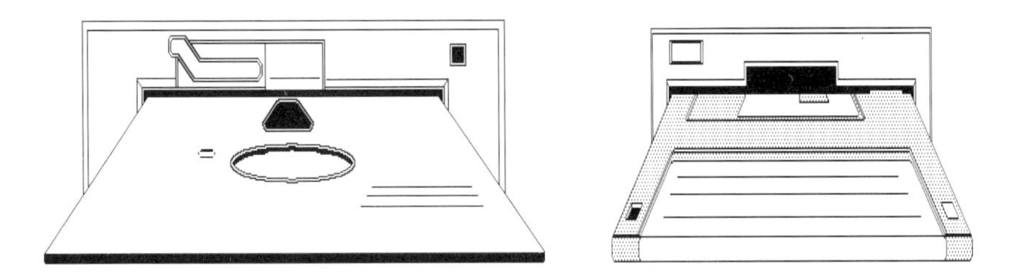

If you have not already bought your PC, then buy one with a 3½" disk drive. This has now become the preferred standard. These disks have greater storage capacity and are better protected with their hard plastic casing. You can have more than one floppy disk drive in your system. Although for most applications, a hard disk and one floppy disk drive is quite adequate.

5¼ " disk

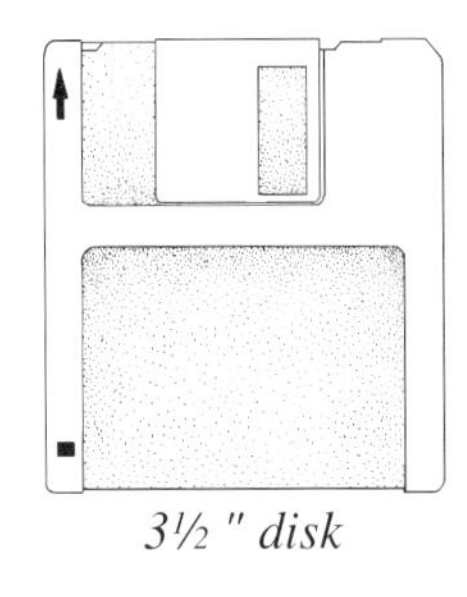

3½ " disk

The storage capacity of disks can be measured in bytes. One byte is equivalent to one character. A kilobyte is 1024 bytes or characters and it is abbreviated as K or Kb. A 5¼" floppy disk can store 360K or 1.2Mb (Mb is a thousand kilobytes or approximately 1 million bytes). A 3½" disk can usually store 360K, 720K or 1.44Mb.

We have looked at the basic components of PCs. Some of the other peripheral parts that are added to the PC to make it more useful or easier to use are:

- Printer
- Mouse
- Scanner

Printer

Although the printer is not the main part of your PC, it is very unlikely that you will be able to do without it. Printers allow you to produce "hardcopies" of your work. If you are using your PC for writing letters, you will need a printer to produce them on paper. If you are working on business applications such as accounting, you will need to print reports from it at some stage.

There are many choices for printers. The best way to understand the pros and cons of printers is to look at the way they work.

Daisy Wheel

These work in the same way as typewriters. Inside the printer there is a wheel, very similar to a bicycle spindle. At the end of each spindle a character is embossed. To print a character the wheel spins until the character is in place, and then the printer impresses the character onto the ribbon, and an image is created on paper. The main advantage of these printers is that the print quality is just as good as that of typewriters. Daisy wheel printers are often called *letter-quality* printers.

The major drawback is that they are noisy and very slow (18 - 55 characters per second) compared to other printers. There is not a lot you can do about the speed. You can, however, buy printer acoustic cases to reduce the noise.

Dot Matrix

These printers are usually low-priced and used widely. The print heads contain either 9 or 24 pins. To print a character, the printer hammers these pins at the ribbon, creating dots on the paper, in the shape of the character. You can easily recognise output from a dot matrix printer - the characters are made of several tiny dots.

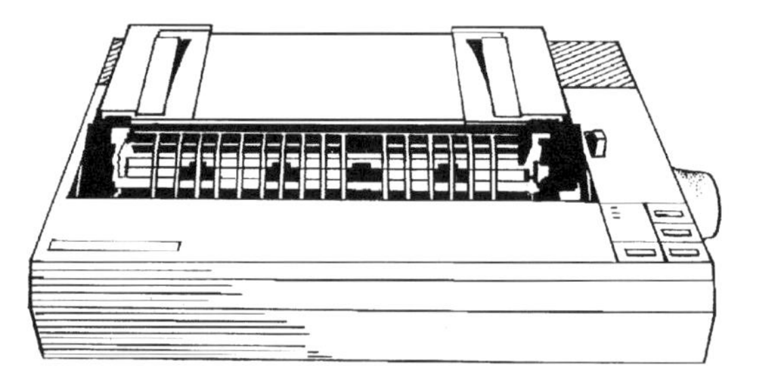

Dot Matrix Printer

The print quality of 24-pin printers is much finer, but 9-pin printers are cheaper. The best quality output you can get from dot matrix printers is called *"near letter quality"* (NLQ); produced by 24-pin printers. The 9-pin printers achieve NLQ by printing repeatedly until the dots are joined-up, but this slows down the speed drastically. And it is the speed that separates low-end models from higher ones. Speed can vary from about 180 characters per second (cps) to over 360 cps.

Dot Matrix printers are ideal for printing on continuous stationery. For example, invoices, labels and so on. You can even use multi-part paper. They are not recommended for high quality printing.

Laser

Neither of the printers discussed so far are designed to print graphics. Laser printers are quite popular in business today because they produce impressive documents with graphical charts.

Although pricey, they can produce high print quality - almost as good as typesetting. Hence, the term "*near typeset quality*" is used to describe output from laser printers.

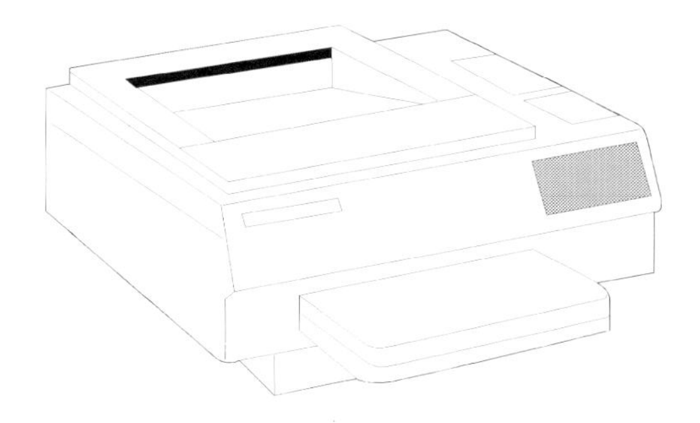

Laser printer

These printers use laser technology to create characters and shapes on paper. They work in a similar way to photocopiers, whereby an image is copied a page at a time. Unlike other printers, where a character is processed one at a time, laser printers process a whole page at a time. Therefore the printing speed for laser printers is measured in pages per minute.

As well as the excellent print quality, laser printers are fast and very quiet - and usually cost more than other types of printers. If you are going to use your PC to produce impressive documents then you should acquire a laser printer. Lower end laser printers (300 dots per inch resolution) have come down in price considerably.

Ink Jet

These printers work like dot matrix printers, but instead of shooting pins against the ribbon, they shoot a fine jet of ink and therefore do not need ribbons. You can also have different colour inks. Ink-jet printers cannot produce a very high quality print.

Bubble Jet

These are one of the later additions to low-cost printers introduced to the market. The basic technology used here is very similar to that used by ink jet printers. The print heads in the bubble jet printers contain thin nozzles, which hold ink. They also have a heating component. When you start a print job, the heating component produces bubbles that expand and fire the ink at the paper. Again, because of non-mechanical techniques used to print, these printers are very quiet. The quality is also pretty good.

If your budget is limited and you need to produce impressive documents, bubble jet printers are good alternatives to laser printers. They cost a lot less.

Mouse

A mouse is an optional input device that is becoming more and more popular. Most of the software being developed today allows you to use a mouse. If your work is going to involve a lot of cursor movements, when drawing for instance, then you should definitely use a mouse. The mouse makes cursor-control a lot easier and faster.

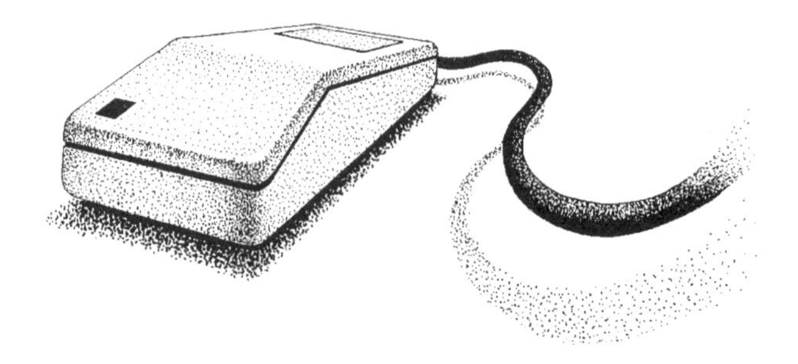

Mouse

The mouse is placed on your desk, usually on top of a 'mouse mat', next to your keyboard. To move the cursor using a mouse, just move your mouse up, down, left or right and then click when the little arrow on your screen is in the right position.

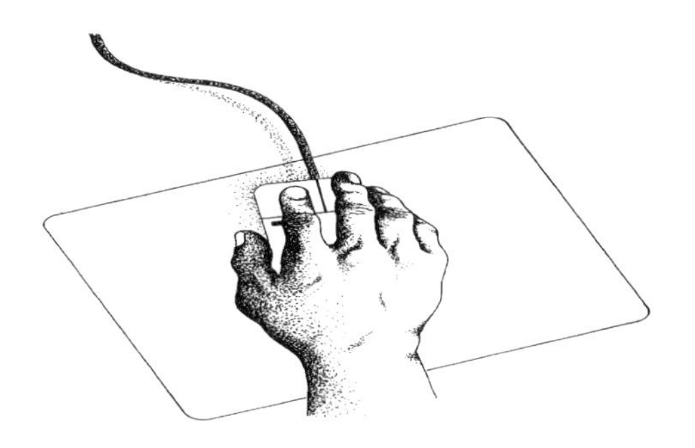

Driving a Mouse on a mouse mat

There are two technical standards for the PC mouse within the industry: Microsoft and Mouse Systems. The former standard is becoming the dominant one. So when you get a mouse make sure that it is Microsoft-Compatible.

Scanner

Scanners use the technology of facsimile machines. They read an image from paper and instead of sending it down the telephone line, they convert the image into a format that your PC can understand. The computer holds the image as a graphics file, which you can print, amend or add to other documents.

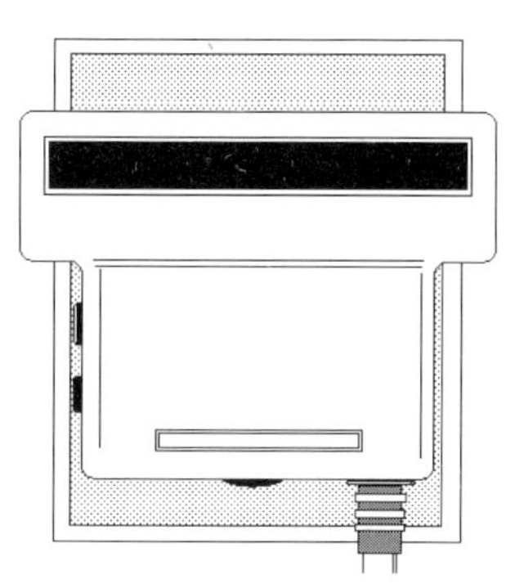

Scanner

You will need a scanner if you want to include pictures, such as photographs, in your document. For the best resolution, buy a flat-bed scanner. Hand-held ones are cheaper, but the quality of pictures produced is not as good. Check the resolution of images generated by a scanner before buying it.

Types of PCs

Confused by the wide range of PCs on the market? The main thing to realise is that all PCs are just expensive calculators - all made to perform the same functions.

What varies between various models is the speed, capacity and portability. Obviously, the faster a PC can process data, the more it is going to cost. If you are going to use a PC for serious applications then you will need one that can cope with large amounts of data. If you need to use a PC from various locations then you will want to buy a lightweight portable.

The major part of the PC that determines its capabilities is the micro chip used for its processor. When looking at a PC specification you will notice the term MHz listed as part of the processor type. E.g. 80386SX (16 MHz). This is the actual speed rating given to the chip. MHz stands for MegaHertz and means millions of pulses per second. Hence, 16 MHz means 16 million pulses per second. A PC has an internal clock that sends out millions of pulses per second. Each instruction executed by a PC uses up several pulses but the higher the number of pulses per second, the faster the PC can execute the instruction. So a 80386 with 20 MHz will be faster than a 80386 with 16 MHz.

The first broad classification of PCs on the market is:

- Desktop PCs - designed to be placed on your desk and expected to remain there for most of the time.
- Portable PCs - aims to satisfy users who are on the move a lot and need a PC that they can move around easily.

Desktop

The first IBM PC was a desktop and based on the 8088 chip. It was a basic PC with two floppy disk drives. Today an ordinary PC uses a 8086 chip. It may or may not have a hard disk. If it has a hard disk, it is also known as an XT.

Moving upwards, the next PC model uses a 80286 chip. The IBM 80286 was first launched in 1984. It is also known as an AT or simply a 286 PC. An AT usually has a hard disk. The basic improvement offered by this model over the XT model is in memory. As a result of more memory with this model and its improved memory management capabilities, the AT, unlike the XT enables you to have more than one program in memory. Although these are still widely used today, they aren't powerful enough for running advanced applications.

In 1986, Compaq launched a PC using a more powerful 80386 chip. This model is faster than the AT. The main attraction of the 386 model is that it can carry on with certain background jobs, such as printing, whilst the user is working on the main application. However, it is more expensive than a 286 and needs more RAM to cope with the 'multitasking' feature.

To overcome the problem of price, a cheaper version of 80386 chip was introduced, known as 80386SX. The original 80386 model is now known as 80386DX. The 80386SX PC can process data almost as fast as the original 80386 and cost just a little more than the 80286 model. Internally both the chips are identical. The major difference between the two is realised when transmitting data from one PC to another. The 80386DX can transmit data nearly twice as fast as the 80386SX. The 80386SX PC is more popular than the 80386DX. Nevertheless, the 80386DX PC is still widely used for large applications and when it needs to be connected to a *network*.

In 1989, Intel introduced 80486 chips for the PC. The 486 model was really designed for the power users. It is two to three times faster than the 386 and used to be much more expensive. However, prices have been plummeting and now the 486 is the best seller.

Just arriving on the market are PCs based on the 586 chipset. You will find that these are extremely fast and exciting to use, but do you really need one?

Still under the category of desktop PCs, there is the PS/2 (Personal System /2) range. IBM introduced the PS/2 range in 1987, targetting it at the power users in businesses. The PS/2 range is based on different technology from the PC range and replaces many chips (bought in from other manufacturers) inside the computer, although the main chip used for the processor is still from the 8088 family. IBM tried to use the PS/2 series to introduce yet another operating system standard, OS/2. So PS/2 can work under already established operating system DOS and also the new OS/2. OS/2 gives true multitasking and other improved facilities. However, due to lack of software available to work with this operating system and general user resistence to move away from DOS, the future of OS/2 remains uncertain.

Within the PS/2 range, all models offer sophisticated features such as VGA screens and enhanced keyboards. The PS/2 range is quite popular with corporate users - probably because it is by IBM.

Having failed in the home market in its first attempt with PC-Junior, IBM tried again with the introduction of PS/1. The first PS/1 model was based on the 286 chip and came with a VGA 12" screen offering reasonable resolution. Now there are several PS/1 models with a higher specification. The PS/1 range is aimed at individuals and small businesses. PS/1 is quite expensive for most home computer users, but, it comes with all sorts of software consisting of a word processor, database, spreadsheet, communications and menu-driven general house-keeping routines.

You can not write a book on computers in the UK without covering the Amstrad PC - the PC for the masses. Amstrad became a major player in the computer industry with its PCW - a personal computer dedicated to word processing. The first IBM PC clone it introduced was PC1512. This was the cheapest PC in the UK and became very popular with small companies and private users. Since then Amstrad has been trying to go upmarket to be accepted by the larger companies. It introduced the PC2000 range in 1988. Unfortunately, the early batches of the range came with technical problems and faults that did not help the company's aim of getting into the corporate market.

Amstrad tried again with the launch of the PC 3000 (Generation 3) range. With all the technical problems of the 2000 series eliminated, this range leaves little excuse for non-acceptance by corporates. The PC 3000s were also the first Amstrad PCs to have metal casing. Since then, Amstrad has followed with the Generation 4, 5, 6 and 7 series.

Portable

The portable PC has evolved over the years from the peripheral printer, known as HX20 manufactured by Epson. HX20 was a point-of-sale terminal that had a keyboard and ran on batteries.

Today we have a variety of portable PCs with full desktop PC power. They are based on the same microprocessors as the desktop PC. Just like all other hardware, portables are falling in prices. Portables in the market today fall under three basic categories:

Notebook

By definition a notebook should be the same length and width as the standard A4 size paper, but obviously quite a bit thicker. It should be able to fit in a standard briefcase. Present day notebooks do, but leave little room for anything else you may wish to carry. Notebooks run from the mains or on rechargeable batteries, lasting from 2 to 4 hours depending on how hard it has to work to process your data. Frequent floppy disk accesses, for instance, will use more battery power. The keyboards have fewer keys than the standard PC keyboard. Some keys are used for more than one character. Most notebooks weigh around 3 kilograms.

Laptop

A laptop weighs around the seven kilogram mark and is quite a bit bigger than the notebook. It usually comes with its own case, which is about two thirds of the size of a standard briefcase. Like a notebook, a laptop runs either from the mains or from rechargeable batteries. The major advantage of the laptop over the notebook is its expansion capabilities. You can upgrade your laptop easily with extra hardware to use it as a fax or to communicate with other PCs.

Laptop computer

Transportable

This type of portable PC is generally heavier than the other two. Although designed to be easily moveable, it is certainly not designed to be carried for a long time. It weighs around ten kilograms and it only runs from the mains. It usually comes with a lot more RAM and is comparable to top-end desktop PCs.

Software Solutions

Software is the most important part of a computer system. It enables you to draft a letter, perform calculations or manage your information. Your computer or hardware is of little use without software. A computer system without software is like a complete music system, including speakers and amplifier, but without any music tapes or records. Your music system can be very sophisticated and expensive, but without any music to play on it, it is of little use.

So what is software exactly? It is a program or a collection of programs written to enable your computer to perform a useful task. A program is made up of special commands and statements that are obeyed and executed by your computer. A computer cannot do anything that it has not been programmed to do.

Types of Software

There are thousands of commercial software packages available for the PC today. They range from simple games programs to complex applications. New and better software packages are being developed every day. We will look at the main categories of software in this section and discuss the important features and benefits they offer.

The main categories of software are:

- Word Processors
- Spreadsheets
- Databases
- Accounting
- Graphics
- Desktop Publishing
- Integrated Software
- Utilities
- Specialised Software

Word Processors

A PC-based word processor package is far superior to the traditional typewriter. Even the market for expensive dedicated word processor machines, was wiped out almost overnight, after general word processing software came on the scene. Today there are many individuals and companies purchasing PCs primarily for creating documents.

Word processors are different because you can easily change your text as often as you want before printing the final document. You can edit on-screen, reposition blocks of text, specify automatic centering or straight right margin, search for specific words and replace them automatically, create a standard header and a footer (with page numbers, say), and so on.

As well as the standard facilities mentioned above, better and more advanced word processors offer other features like:

Spell Checker

Checks either all your spellings or specific words against an online dictionary.

Thesaurus

Allows you to see synonyms (words with similar meanings) so that you can decide on words best suited.

Auto-save

Saves your document onto disk automatically at a given time interval. This is especially important if you are typing in a long document and don't want to risk losing it all.

Mail-merge

Enables you to combine two files. It is usually used to merge a file containing names and addresses with a standard letter to create personalised letters.

WYSIWYG

Pronounced "wizzy-wig". It stands for "what you see is what you get" and means that when you use special printing effects like **bold** and underlining, you'll be able to see these on the screen exactly as they appear when printed.

Print Preview

Sometimes called page preview. It allows you to see the complete page with all the formatting including margins, headers and footers, on one screen. It saves you wasting paper and time because you know what your printed page is going to look like before you commit yourself to printing it.

Macros

If you need to type the same long piece of text, or you need to perform the same key operations frequently, you can specify these once in a macro. Then, assign a function key, like F12, to your macro. Every time you want to repeat the sequence of commands or to type the same piece of text, simply press F12.

Indexing and Table of Contents

Advanced word processors can automatically generate a table of contents and an index with page numbers. You can specify or mark the words you want and the word processor will do the rest. If you edit your document, you can simply ask your word processor to regenerate the index.

Import and Export

Often there is a requirement to read a file from another word processor or a spreadsheet (importing) and to output the documents you create into other formats (exporting).

A popular word processing package called 'Word for Windows' offers "pull-down" menus which means that all menu options such as File, Edit, Utilities and so on, can be expanded when you click on them with a mouse. You can then easily select the option you require, again with a mouse click, from the pull-down menu.

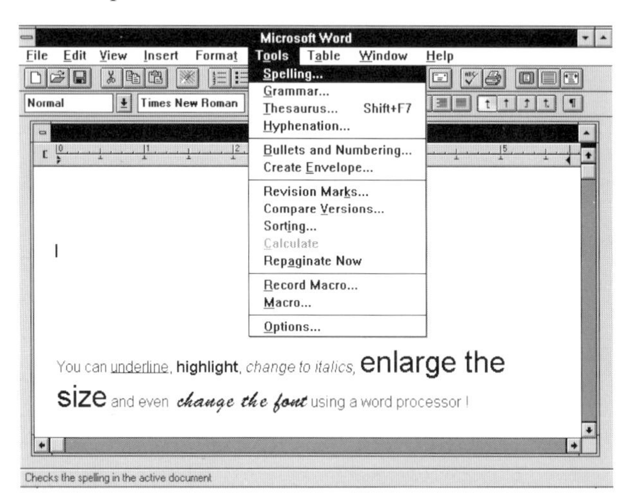

Word for Windows with a pull-down menu to check spellings

Spreadsheets

Lotus 1-2-3 is an example of a spreadsheet and an all-time popular software package. Many businesses and individuals purchased PCs purely to be able to use Lotus 1-2-3.

A spreadsheet can be thought of as a large calculator, used to solve any numerical problem that can be presented in rows and columns. It allows much greater flexibility because you can mix numbers, formulas and text. One great benefit of using a spreadsheet is to be able to perform **"what if"** analysis.

For example, Joe Bloggs wants to arrange a suitable overdraft facility with his bank. Let us assume that purchases are 50% of sales and

	A	B	C	D	E	F	G
1	JOE BLOGGS DISTRIBUTION				CASH FLOW JAN-JUN 1992		
2							
3		Jan-92	Feb-92	Mar-92	Apr-92	May-92	Jun-92
4	OPENING BANK						
5	BALANCE	-3000	-2000	-2600	-2800	200	4800
6							
7	Sales Receipts	10000	6000	7000	15000	19000	24000
8							
9	Purchase Payments	5000	3000	3500	7500	9500	12000
10	Variable Costs Payments	1000	600	700	1500	1900	2400
11	Fixed Costs Payments	3000	3000	3000	3000	3000	3000
12	Total Outflow	9000	6600	7200	12000	14400	17400
13							
14	CLOSING BANK	-2000	-2600	-2800	200	4800	11400
15	BALANCE						

variable costs are 10% of sales. This information can easily be entered in a spreadsheet and derived figures will be calculated automatically, as shown here. We can also see that Joe Bloggs needs to arrange an overdraft facility until April 1992. Now, what if, sales receipts in just the first month were to drop to £5,000. By making this single change, as shown here, the spreadsheet will recalculate all related figures instantly, at a touch of a button. You can also see that the overdraft will be required for an additional month.

	A	B	C	D	E	F	G
1	JOE BLOGGS DISTRIBUTION				CASH FLOW JAN-JUN 1992		
2							
3		Jan-92	Feb-92	Mar-92	Apr-92	May-92	Jun-92
4	OPENING BANK						
5	BALANCE	-3000	-4000	-4600	-4800	-1800	2800
6							
7	Sales Receipts	5000	6000	7000	15000	19000	24000
8							
9	Purchase Payments	2500	3000	3500	7500	9500	12000
10	Variable Costs Payments	500	600	700	1500	1900	2400
11	Fixed Costs Payments	3000	3000	3000	3000	3000	3000
12	Total Outflow	6000	6600	7200	12000	14400	17400
13							
14	CLOSING BANK	-4000	-4600	-4800	-1800	2800	9400
15	BALANCE						

This is a very simple example to make the point. You can make it more realistic by incorporating bank interest, breakdown of expenses, breakdown of sales by product and so on. In brief, once you have your raw data in a spreadsheet, you can have any number of scenarios, no matter how complex they might be. You can use a spreadsheet for repetitive accounting tasks or as a tool for management decision making.

Some of the specific features offered by spreadsheets include:

Formulas

All spreadsheets provide simple mathematical operations like subtraction and division from which you can build complex formulas yourself. Most spreadsheets also provide specialised functions and formulas to save you time. These include:

Mathematical	**Average, Count, Maximum, Minimum, Sum**
Trigonometric	**Sine, Cosine, Tangent, Pi**
Logical	**And, Or, Not**
Date	**Date, Time**
Statistical	**Standard Deviation, Variance**
Financial	**Compound interest, Rate of return on investment**

These built-in formulas make it much easier for you to build financial models using your spreadsheet.

Macros

These are very important for automating repetitive procedures within a spreadsheet. You can execute a macro representing several keystrokes or commands by simply pressing a function key. They can speed up your work and make life much easier. Macros can also be used to customise your spreadsheet for specific applications.

Graphics

It is sometimes much easier to understand a single picture or a graph rather than a mass of numbers. Good spreadsheets can instantly create business graphics from basic numerical data. Now your "what if" analysis can not only show the effects numerically, but also graphically.

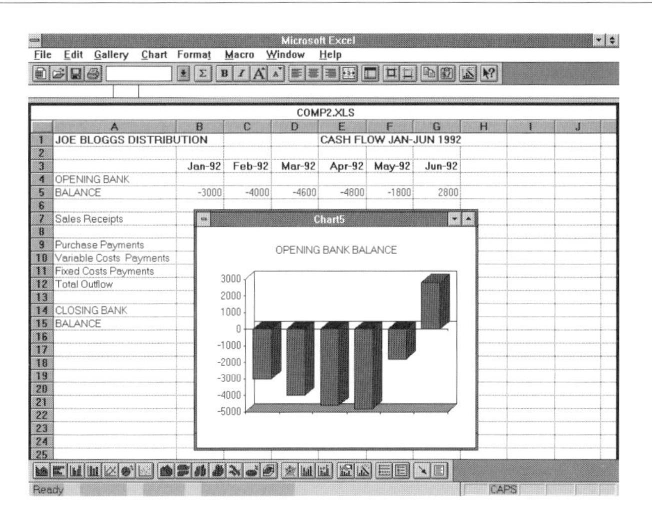

Excel spreadsheet capable of graphics too

Linking

Instead of creating one enormous spreadsheet for the whole company, it is much easier to work with several smaller ones and link them. Changing a value in one spreadsheet will automatically recalculate all related values in other spreadsheets that are linked.

Multi-Dimensional

Say you wanted to record Sales by Salesmen and by Area. Normally, you'd have to create two spreadsheets; one for Sales by Salesmen and another one for Sales by Area and then link them. An alternative is to create one three-dimensional spreadsheet to record Sales, Salesmen and Area details. You can then even produce a three-dimensional graph from it.

Databases

A database is a collection of data, called a file, stored in a computer. Examples include mailing lists, customer records and employee data. A database management system (DBMS), commonly called a database too, is a software package allowing you to store, manipulate and retrieve data. A database is different from a spreadsheet because it allows you to record the current 'real' state of your business rather t future projections.

A database is often described as an electronic card-file. A database record is equivalent to a card. The individual pieces of information on a card, like name, address, telephone number, are known as fields within a record. Databases that replicate the card-file exactly are known as flat-file databases.

The real power of databases is only realised in a relational database management system (RDBMS). A relational database package allows you to have many tables or databases - each capable of joining with another to provide powerful cross-referencing. It also avoids duplication of data. Relational databases are more sophisticated and expensive. Almost every database software supplier has jumped on the 'relational-band-wagon' - claiming to be offering a relational solution. It is therfore wise, when choosing your system, to look closely at the features offered, rather than relying solely on the relational label.

Some of the main features to look for include:

Ease of Use

It must be easy to create and modify databases. You should also be able to input new information and display it easily.

Indexing

This is a way of accessing a record or several records within a large database quickly. It is a technique similar to the one we use when we search the index of a book to find the relevant pages. In the database context, a new file is created and it represents an index to the main database file.

Relations

Quite often you will need to create several files; and link them with a relation. A relation is where there is a record in each file with common attributes and so a link can be formed. An example is a customer file forming a relation with an orders file on customer number.

Manipulation

Once you have created your database and entered information in it, you need a facility to manipulate the data to reap maximum benefits. This is done by:

- functions like COUNT, MAXIMUM, MINIMUM to operate on the data. These are similar to those provided in a spreadsheet.
- a programming environment. The standard PC database programming language is DBASE.
- a facility to submit queries to the database. A standard query language is SQL (Structured Query Language). Some packages offer a Query-By-Example facility too. This is a simple form on your screen that you fill and the query is automatically generated from it.

Screens and Menus

It is fine to use the default screen to input data initially. However, it is much better to be able to design your own screens for data-entry and manipulation. You should be able to place fields anywhere on the screen, draw boxes, type headings and so on. Customised menus will allow you to use different parts of your system and link your screens together.

Reports and Labels

A report generator should allow you to format your report easily. You should be able to test the report with a print preview before printing it on paper. A label generator is a common requirement from a database. You should be able to specify the format of your labels and again print preview them with actual data before committing to final printing.

As well as the facilities above, check that it is easy to make changes to the structure of your database, even after you have entered data.

The database should not slow down as you input more data and it should offer on-screen help.

Choosing the right database package to start with is perhaps more important than for any other type of software. This is because once you have created your complete application (screens, reports, programs), and input data, it is difficult to make major changes or to make it conform to another database software package. Many database software companies provide a demonstration disk of virtually the full product, so that you can evaluate their product thoroughly before making a decision to buy it. You are just limited in the number of records you can create.

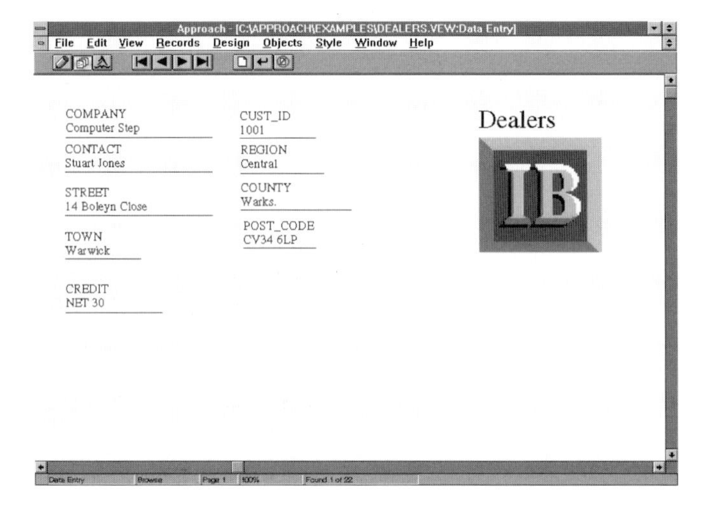

Approach for Windows is an easy-to-use DBMS

Approach for Windows has VCR-like buttons to browse through records. You can also easily redesign the form layout, edit the information and search for records by providing part data.

Accounting

An accounting system is one application of a database system. It is possible to write your own accounting system from a database if you are technically inclined and have the time. For most, it is far easier to purchase an off-the-shelf accounts package.

It is also possible to use a spreadsheet, especially for small businesses, rather than to buy a full blown accounts system. If, however, you have to have a proper accounts system, then the choice is very wide. Most offer Sales, Purchase and Nominal ledgers. Other facilities to look for include:

- Invoice production and credit note facility
- Bank payment and petty cash
- Reports: VAT return, account history, debt-chasing letters, budgets, audit trial, Profit and Loss report, Balance sheet.

Quite often you can also purchase additional modules if you need to extend the basic accounting system. Examples include stock control, Job costing and Payroll. If you purchase a payroll system you should make sure that you will receive updates whenever the Government changes PAYE and NIC regulations.

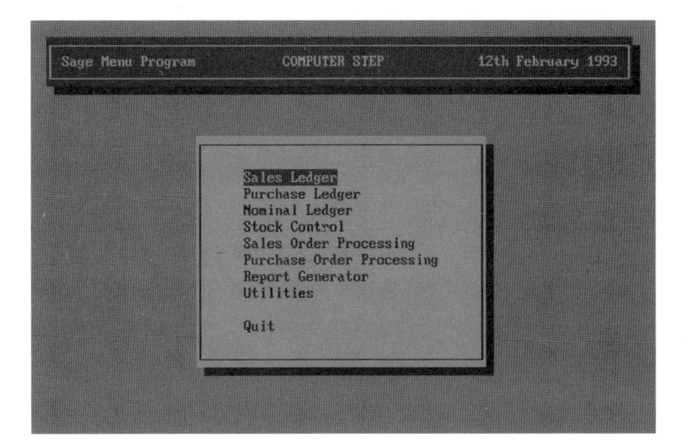

Sage - An example of a computerised accounting system

Graphics

Graphics is increasingly becoming more and more important on PCs. Many word processors, spreadsheets and databases offer a graphics capability. However, they are limited in functionality. If you want a proper graphics facility, you may need to buy an appropriate graphics package.

There are many different types of graphic packages. To understand the benefits and functions they can offer, we will split them into four basic types. These are:

- Business
- Drawing and Painting
- Presentation
- CAD

Business

These packages allow you to produce standard business graphs. They include Bar charts, Pie charts, X-Y line graphs and so on. Check that the software will accept data from your spreadsheet or database, otherwise you may have to type the numbers in again. Many of these products can also display 3D graphs.

Drawing and Painting

These packages are a substitute for either a pencil or a paintbrush. They allow you to create free-hand line drawings (Drawing programs) and you can fill an area with colour (Painting programs).

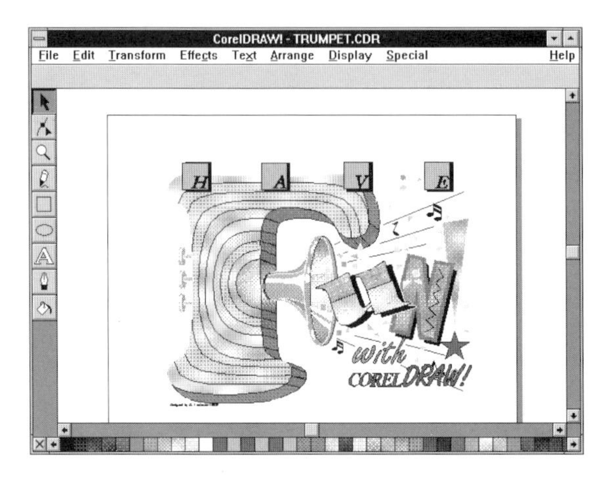

CorelDraw is a well known drawing package

Since most of us are not artists, these paages often come with a library of cliparts. These are drawings already created by someone else. You can simply copy them and make modifications if necessary.

Presentation

These packages specialise in producing graphics on overhead projector foils or on 35mm photographic slides. You can even turn your PC into a slide projector - each picture will be displayed in turn on your screen after a key-press or a short time delay.

CAD

These are special types of programs used for complex technical drawings. It stands for Computer Aided Design.

If precision and accuracy are very important than a CAD program is required. Examples of use include designing a car or a building.

Desktop Publishing

Desktop Publishing (DTP) is a way of integrating text and graphics on the same page. DTP will allow you to use your PC for producing high quality brochures, newsletters, books, magazines and other types of documents.

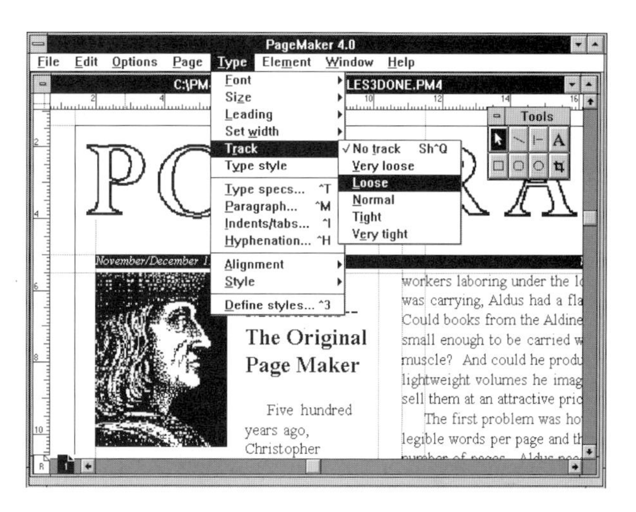

PageMaker is a leading DTP package

DTP on the PC today is far more cost effective than traditional typesetting. It saves countless hours on manual cut-and-paste, corrections and general layout. To get into DTP, the most important requirement is choosing the right software. DTP software on its own, however, will not do everything. You will still need a word processor for typing in the text; a graphics package, and perhaps a scanner if you need to scan pictures or images into your document.

When choosing DTP software, make sure it is compatible with other software and hardware you plan to use with it. You may also decide to invest in a laser printer for high-quality output.

Some important features that DTP software can offer include:

Drop Cap

This is a large capital letter occupying several lines. It is usually used to start the first paragraph in a chapter, as seen in this book.

Grid

This is an area defined to lay out an object. DTP software can automatically align text or graphics to fit inside this grid.

Kerning

Allows you to close-up letters so that they almost overlap. This can make large important headlines easier to read.

Tracking

Automatically reduces spacing between letters and words in the main body of the text.

Integrated Software

Instead of buying a separate software package for each function you can just buy one integrated package. An integrated package can provide a combination of the following:

- Word Processor
- Spreadsheet
- Database
- Communication
- Graphics
- Desktop accesories (such as calculator, diary)

Examples include Microsoft Works and Lotus Works. They provide major cost savings when compared to buying the individual packages. However, integrated packages cannot compete with the best word processors, spreadsheets and databases in the market.

Utilities

Utility software enables you to work with your PC more easily. You can have a utility to:

- Backup and Restore files
- Recover corrupted files
- Organise your hard disk
- Encrypt or protect important files

Some utilities just perform one task, whilst others may perform a combination of chores.

Specialised Software

There are many specialised packages that don't fit into any of the above categories. You can usually find software to help you with just about anything. For example, how about improving your writing with Grammatik? This useful package is designed to check your grammar as well as writing-style. It works with most popular word processors and allows you to make corrections interactively. A special British edition of this American product is also available.

Or perhaps you want to plan your road journey on a PC using Autoroute. Autoroute is another useful package that provides a map of any journey. It can also present alternative routes so that you may pick the shortest distance, the most economical or the quickest time to get from one place to another. You can then demand a detailed table of driving directions.

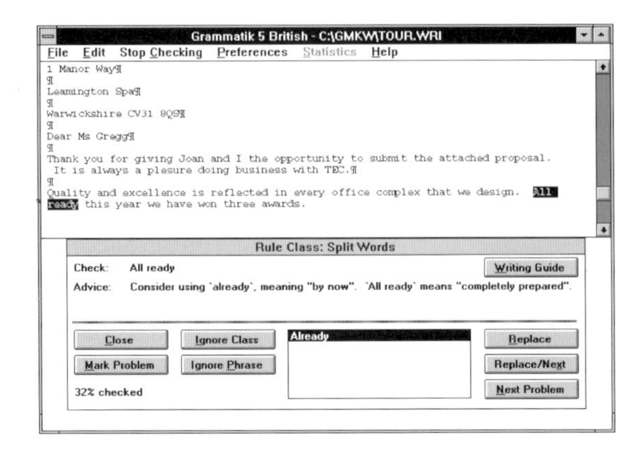

Grammatik claims to detect over 10,000 writing errors

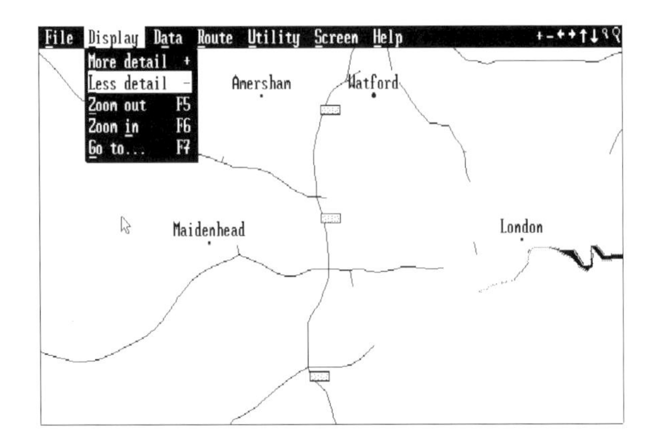

An example of a journey map in Autoroute

Shareware and Public Domain

Shareware is an interesting marketing concept used to promote sales of software. It allows you to try the software before you decide to buy it. All you need to pay initially is a few pounds for the disk and handling. Basic documentation on how to use the program is provided as a file on the same disk. You are trusted to register the program if you decide to keep on using it. Once you have paid the registration fee, you will normally receive an upgraded version of the product, full documentation manuals and technical support.

Public Domain (PD) software is slightly different. You can use it as often as you please without ever paying any money to the authors.

Beware of Viruses

A computer virus is a man-made electronic disease. It can corrupt files on your PC and wipe off important data. It can strike anytime. Even when you least expect it.

So what is a virus exactly? It is a piece of software designed to cause severe destruction to important information on your PC. It is often designed to be transmitted easily from one PC to another without being detected. This spreading of viruses is particularly easy if your PC is linked to others, or if you use floppy disks for information exchange.

To detect viruses and to kill them, you can buy anti-virus toolkits. However, none can guarantee to detect all viruses - new ones are continuously produced. Other precautions you should take include:

- Do not try software from dubious sources
- Be careful who you let loose on your PC
- Take regular backups of your data and software

Let's Go Shopping

This chapter takes you through the stages involved in choosing and buying your hardware and software - in other words, your system. It also gives you detailed guidelines on using various sources for finding relevant information before making a purchasing decision.

To choose the right system you should consider the following steps:

Why a PC?

Before you venture out any further, work out in your mind why exactly you want to buy a PC. It is quite surprising how many people buy a PC without having a clear idea about what they want to do with it. Then they get disappointed when they realise that their machine is not powerful enough to run the software they need. Do you want a PC for a serious application such as wordprocessing or accounting for your business? Do you want a PC for entertainment purposes or do you want to buy a PC for educational purposes? Perhaps you want a PC for all of these reasons. For instance, you may want a word processor at home for writing letters and some educational software for your children. But, your spouse rather likes the idea of playing a game of golf on it. Perhaps you also have a more specialised requirement such as composing music.

What's available?

Once you have identified why you want a PC, you need to find out what is available in the market to meet your requirements. The latter part of this chapter looks at how to find information on various products. This section discusses the factors to consider when looking through this information:

Features

Study and compare all the features offered by competing products. Do they provide all the features you may need? Do any of the products offer any exceptional features?

Price

Obviously, the more sophisticated a product is the higher the price tag. A laser printed output is quite attractive, but do you really need it to write letters to your bank manager. Similarly, the latest version of WordPerfect is not a necessity if you are just going to use your PC to write formal letters. However, if you are buying a PC to write a book or to write customer proposals, then, your minimum requirements may be a laser printer and an advanced word processor.

Compatibility

As mentioned in the last chapter, software is the most important part of your system. First, you need to decide on the software packages you intend using. Then, find out their minimum system requirements. These will include factors such as: memory, hard disk and processing speed. Make sure that the hardware you buy will easily be able to run all your software. You also need to allow for extra hard disk storage for your data.

Learning curve

The more advanced a product is, the longer it takes to learn to use it. Some of the expensive software offer advanced features. However, simple functions may be difficult to find and use. You may want to buy software that is familiar to you. If you are buying a PC to do extra work at home, you may want to buy the same software that you use at work to shorten your learning curve.

Reliability

When buying a PC for serious business applications, avoid computer hardware that has been known to have problems. Software does not suddenly fail, but it may contain 'bugs'. A software bug is when the program does not behave as expected in certain circumstances. For serious applications, such as business accounting, avoid first releases of new products, unless they have been available for quite some time. With complex applications it takes quite a while before all the bugs are found and eliminated. Although these bugs are not always serious, as a new computer user you want to steer clear from all known problems, no matter how minor they may be.

Budgeting

Once you have a fair idea of how much a personal computer system can cost, you can plan how much you want to spend on each individual part. When budgeting, start with the essentials. For a small business, these may be: an accounting software package that can generate invoices, a printer that allows you to print on continuous stationery and a PC with 40 megabyte hard disk. Work out how much these items will cost. Add the cost of small accessories like printer cables. If you have any funds left in your budget, then you can go for little luxuries such as a higher resolution screen.

Obtaining the best deal

Getting the best deal means finding a good price as well as reasonable support. Don't just look for the lowest price. Look for a reliable and helpful supplier. Check that all products carry a vendor's warranty against defects in workmanship. Generally, computer hardware is guaranteed for twelve months against any faults that may develop and technical problems you may encounter. Whereas, with software you generally get free technical support for a few months. After this period you have to buy your support.

If you buy the total system from one company you may be able to negotiate a good price or get some freebies. Be careful when a computer dealer tells you that he is giving you free software with your computer. Quite often computer manufacturers bundle popular software with their PCs. Check that the dealer is giving away what he claims.

When it comes to finding information on computer products, you want to start from independent sources (i.e. those who do not sell computer products), such as product reviews in computer magazines. Your friends and colleagues can also be good independent sources - if they don't sell computers for a living. Once you are fairly confident with the lingo and know how to compare different products, then approach computer dealers for detailed information and advice.

Use these sources to choose (and buy) your computer system:

Computer Magazines

The next step after reading this book is to find information on various computer products. Start by reading leading computer magazines. Do this even before you approach your local dealer. Although you will need to spend some time reading, you will avoid getting confused by computer dealers or being misled into buying the wrong system.

Types available

The main categories of PC magazines for end users can be defined by the type of readers they are aimed at:

General consumers and beginners
These magazines cover issues concerning all PC users. They can be purchased at most newsagents.

Professionals in large organisations
These look at issues relating specifically to large companies. Most are available by free subscriptions to anyone with an authority to purchase systems or to influence purchasing decisions within an organisation.

Small/medium size business owners

These are available by subscriptions only. As well as covering topics relating to PCs, these magazines cover various business issues.

Technical users

Covers technical topics such as programming.

For your purpose of choosing a computer system, magazines available in newsagents are appropriate.

Product reviews

One main function of these magazines is to review all major products being released in the market. Most reviews are independent from product vendors. Unlike your local computer dealers, the magazine writers when reviewing products, are not trying to sell to you. Also, because they see and review many products, they are able to provide a fair judgement.

Product reviews usually consist of a detailed description of the features offered by the product, followed by the reviewer's opinion and general ratings on factors such as ease of use, functionality, documentation, speed and value for money. More useful reviews also provide a comparison between competing products. Almost all reviews state where to get more information or where to buy the products.

To play it safe, you should read at least two or three reviews on a specific product. You may also contact the vendors to obtain copies of reviews on their products. They will be pleased to send you these, especially if the reviews are favourable. Quite often, it is interesting to read letters that follow a review in subsequent issues. Letters from readers, vendors and competitors often reveal interesting facts that have been overlooked by the reviewer.

Advertisements

Just like advertisements for any other products, advertisements in computer magazines are designed to attract your attention rather than to be informative. Nevertheless, do make a point of looking at these. They will, at least, tell you how to get further information. Almost all ads. have a coupon or a telephone number you can use for further information.

Advertisements can also reveal something about the company and the success of their products. If you see a new ad. in every computer magazine and it disappears after a short time, then it usually means that the campaign was not successful and the product did not achieve anticipated sales. You should perhaps think twice before rushing into buying this product! Also look at the positioning of the ad. Prime positions such as the back cover and front inside cover are the most expensive in the magazine. Usually, it is the larger companies that tend to pay the premium prices for these pages. These companies are more likely to be around for a long time and provide you with support. After these prime positions, come the first few pages of the magazine. These are fairly prominent positions too - and so is the price. Have you ever wondered why the Contents page in magazines is never the first page? Now you know! Magazine publishers are better off selling the page and making it a revenue earner rather than using it themselves.

Some magazines offer a reader enquiry service, whereby you just send off one card to the publishers, indicating the products that interest you from those advertised and reviewed. Using this service to get more information is easier than to write to each individual vendor. Although, it is much slower - be prepared to wait quite a bit longer to receive the details requested.

Some advertisers will encourage you to buy directly from the details provided on an ad. page. This is usually the case with low-priced products. You can usually place orders over the telephone by using a credit card to pay for the purchase.

Other companies that tend to advertise heavily to get your orders over the phone are computer dealers offering leading branded products at reduced prices. Some of these dealers survive by selling very large volumes. They have to put all their efforts into selling, to achieve high unit sales. Therefore, they have less time to provide any technical advice or support. Buy from these dealers once you know what you want.

One thing to remember, when answering these advertisements is that when you request details from companies, your name and address will be added to their customer database. If you use the magazine's reader enquiry service, your details will also be added to the Publisher's database. This is not as bad as it sounds. It allows them to send you updated information on their products. If, however, you are very concerned about receiving "junk- mail", you can ask them not to use the personal details you provide for any other purpose.

Reader Offers

Some consumer computer magazines sell products to their readers at special prices. The magazine publishers act like mail order computer dealers; they buy goods from vendors and sell them to end users. The only difference is that the publishers are much more choosy about the products they sell. The products they offer are typically low-priced and have been recommended in their reviews.

As the term "reader offer" implies, the products are sold at discounted prices to the readers. You send your order by mail; either send a cheque or give your credit card number. Some magazines also offer a telephone ordering service to make it easy for you to order.

Customer support for these products is provided by the vendors. The magazines' reader-offer staff are not really geared towards giving technical advice or resolving technical problems.

So you can use this service to find bargains and feel comfortable that the products you are buying are commendable.

Again, when you buy products from the publisher, or subscribe to their magazine, your details will be maintained on their customer database. So don't be surprised when you regularly start receiving details on subscribing to their other magazines or buying other products. Some publishers also "rent out" their customer database. This means that they give a copy of their customer database, or a selection from it, to other companies at a nominal charge. Companies paying for this list can send a mailshot to addresses on the list once. They cannot take another copy or keep a copy. If they want to use the same list again, they have to make another payment to the list owner. Why would any company want to do this, you may ask? Because they feel that if you buy computer products from reader offers or subscribe to a certain type of publication, you are very likely to purchase their products too.

Exhibitions

Most computer exhibitions tend to be open to trade customers and end users. Although, the organisers do reserve one or two days of the show for business and professional people only.

Computer exhibitions can be useful for fact-finding and for shopping. In the earlier days, most vendors used these shows for demonstration purposes only. Nowadays, to cover their costs of exhibiting, many vendors try to get direct sales at these shows. They will quite often offer their products at lower show prices to encourage customers to place their orders there and then. Several computer dealers also hire stands to sell leading products at low prices.

As a fact-finding venue, the major advantage of attending a computer exhibition is that you can see most branded products under one roof. There are staff present to demonstrate the products and answer any questions you may have. Be careful though, these demonstrators are sales people and may not be very generous in pointing out the limitations of their products. The other major advantage of attending computer exhibitions is that most vendors use these shows to launch new products. Regular visits to computer exhibitions will help you to keep up-to-date with the industry.

To choose your system, as well as knowing who the vendors are, you need to know their status in the industry. At computer shows, company status is very apparent. Companies with the clout in the industry get the most prominent positions - e.g. near the entrance. These companies also have big stands with large company logos. They go out of their way to build special stands with large screens, speakers and whatever else they can add to stand out from other companies. Smaller companies with limited budgets will have standard stands, in peripheral positions such as the sides and the back of the hall.

On entering a computer show, you may get a bit startled by the flashing lights and large, colourful screens everywhere. The way to ensure that your trip here is fruitful is to plan your day before you start. When you register at the entrance you will be offered a Show Guide. For some shows, you can get the show guides earlier by registering in advance. Use these guides to see who is exhibiting what and where. Plan your day carefully so that you can see all the products you want to and still have a couple of hours left to see anything new.

Computer Dealers

In the early eighties, when the PC industry was in its infancy, computer dealers were very profitable. The computer industry was a fast-growing one and offering good profit margins. As a result, everyone and anyone wanted to get into the computing business. Anyone with a slight entrepreneurial flair wanted to jump on the bandwagon. Computer dealers were springing up everywhere - in high streets, local shopping areas and town outskirts. Even electrical retailers were turning into computer dealers! Sadly, most of these rising stars were not interested in computers. They were just keen to make lots of money. So here we are in the nineties, with more outlets selling computers than we need and not many computer dealers able to give us sound advice.

Before visiting a computer dealer, do your homework by reading computer press. Also, learn and understand the basic terminology - a lot of it is explained in this book. Always remember that, if you want to pay the lowest price offered, you will usually not get the best support. To choose a good dealer, talk to friends or colleagues, and find out their experiences of your local dealer.

If there is a specific product you are interested in, call the vendor of that product first. Ask them who they recommend you buy their product from. They will always give you a reputable dealer contact in your area. Also ensure that the dealer is fully authorised to demonstrate and support the product.

Finally, since there are so many makes of computers and related products, most dealers cannot hold large stocks of any one item. Be prepared to place your order and wait a couple of days to pick it up.

High Street Stores

When low-price personal computers, from manufacturers such as Amstrad in the UK, were introduced to the market, the general demand for personal computers was expected to boom. These expectations attracted retail chain stores such as Dixons to join the industry to sell low-end personal computers to consumers and small businesses.

The major attraction of buying your computer from one of these stores is the competitive prices they can offer. An independent dealer generally buys in small volumes and is given the standard trade discounts. High street chain stores can demand high discount from vendors because of their bulk buying nature. Hence, they can afford to pass on some of this discount to their customers.

The major drawback with these stores, is that the shop assistants selling computers tend to be ex-television or ex-vacuum cleaner sales people. If you are lucky, you may be near a larger branch where they have a special "computer centre". Here they should be able to give you proper advice. Although this cannot be guaranteed in all computer centres.

The other limitation with these stores is that they do not deal with all products. They only concentrate on products that are very popular.

To conclude, if you know what you want, and have a standard requirement, then you can take advantage of the low prices offered at these stores.

Computer Supermarkets

This is a fairly new way of shopping. However, it is already an established and a popular concept in the USA. The basic idea is to offer a wide range of hardware, software and accessories under one roof. Like the usual supermarkets, goods are stacked up on shelves and customers just go and pick what they want. To minimise rental costs and to offer a better shopping environment, these stores are located out of central shopping areas and offer ample car parking spaces.

Mail Order

In the computer industry, mail order has become a popular way of shopping.

Firstly, there are the general mail order catalogue companies that offer a wide range of computer products including hardware, software and accessories. These companies have thick catalogues where they list all the products they carry. You can generally get good discounts and free carriage if your order value is substantial. When comparing prices do not forget to add carriage charges. Some mail order companies offer free phone numbers for you to place your orders. Some also offer help lines for general advice. More reputable mail order companies even offer a free warranty against defects in workmanship.

Under the same general category fall computer dealers who also have a back-room mail order business. Some mail order dealers offer unbelievably low prices, especially on software. Check the versions of software they are offering. Quite often these packages are not genuine local versions, but are "grey-imports" from another country.

Grey imports in the computer industry are products which are designed and priced to be used in the country of origin, but have been exported to another country, without the approval of vendors. American versions, for instance, are normally priced much lower than the UK versions. Hence, the UK dealer can afford to sell them at attractive prices. However, try and resist the temptation of buying these products - you will not get technical support from the vendors' local offices or favourably priced upgrades for your software.

The other type of mail order company is the product vendor who sells directly to the end customer by mail. With some vendors, such as Dell, you can buy their products directly. These manufacturers claim that by selling direct rather than through computer dealers they can offer lower prices. They can save the middleman's profits, and pass them onto you. They also claim that, this way they can have a direct relationship with their customers and provide better technical support. This is quite true with some of these companies. Dell's technical support, for instance, is rated quite highly in the industry. However, not all computer vendors selling direct can be rated so favourably.

Some mail order companies do not advertise but send details of their products or services directly to you by post. They usually obtain your details by renting a customer list from magazine publishers (as discussed under Reader Offers) or other companies from whom you may have purchased something.

If you choose to buy your computer, software or other accessories by mail or telephone, it is wiser to use a credit card rather than sending a cheque. Should you have a dispute with the supplier, or should the company suddenly disappear and you have not received your goods, it may then be possible for you to get the credit card company to help you resolve the matter or provide you with a refund.

The other factor to look out for when buying by mail is whether the company offers a moneyback guarantee, should the product be unsuitable. You will usually find advertisements offering "30 Days Moneyback Guarantee".

When you have bought your new computer system check that all the parts are delivered and intact. Check that everything is working. If you have any problems, contact your supplier immediately.

Complete and send all the registration cards to the appropriate vendors straightaway. If you fail to register, you may have problems getting support. Also, with software, you will not qualify for upgrades at special prices, often offered to existing registered customers.

DOS and all that Jazz

A computer is an extremely fast and efficient machine, but it is just that - a machine. It cannot think for itself and needs to be told exactly what to do. A simple operation, such as copying a file involves the computer needing several instructions like find the file, read it, find empty space on the disk to write the new file, and so on. If you had to give your PC so many detailed commands every time you wanted to perform a simple operation, you would find it very cumbersome and time-consuming. You will probably give-up using your PC altogether. In order to make life a little easier, a special language exists to translate your copy command, and many others like it, into detailed instructions that control various components, like the disks, memory, monitor, and so on. This language is called DOS.

What is DOS?

DOS stands for Disk Operating System. After you switch on your PC, DOS will attempt to interpret anything you type on your almost blank screen. If you type one of the commands that exists within it's library (see later for an explanation and syntax of some basic DOS commands), then DOS will execute your request. If, however, DOS does not find your command, it will look for a program with the same name, and if that exists, it will automatically be loaded into the RAM and executed. If nothing is found matching your command, DOS will issue a message:

```
Bad command or file name
```

DOS consists of several program files and it is always stored on a hard disk, if you have one. If you don't have a hard disk, DOS will be held on a floppy - often called the *system disk*. The files comprising DOS programs are called the *system files*.

DOS is the most popular *systems software* for the PC. Others you may hear of are: DR DOS, OS/2, and Concurrent DOS. As a beginner you should stick to DOS. Because of its popularity, more software is developed to work with DOS and it is likely to be around for a long time.

There are two types of DOS: MS-DOS and PC-DOS. Both versions are developed by Microsoft, a leading software company. PC-DOS was written specifically for IBM to be used with the IBM PC. MS-DOS is almost like PC-DOS and it is used with all IBM PC compatibles, or clones. And since there are more clones being sold than IBM PCs, MS-DOS is more widely used.

DOS is a very powerful tool. It enables you to take full advantage of what your PC can do. So don't put off learning DOS any longer. Just take a deep breath and follow the next few pages to grasp the basic essentials. The basic commands described here will be valid regardless of the version of DOS you have. Even future versions, like MS-DOS 6, will allow you to use the same commands.

The System Prompt

When your PC is waiting for your instructions or commands, it will display what is called a system prompt on your screen. It looks like:

C>   if you have a hard disk

or `A>` if you just have floppy disk system

You can customise the prompt to make it more useful. For example, type,

```
C> prompt $p$g ↵
```

This command will enable you to see not only the disk drive, but also the directory (see later for how to create and change directories). For example:

`C:\>`	If you are in the main directory, called the root.
`C:\ACCOUNTS>`	If you are in a directory called ACCOUNTS

The *PROMPT* command can also be used to always display the date and time. If you want to see today's date, use $d. Likewise, the current time will always be shown if you include $t in the *PROMPT* command. You may even want to see a special message, like "Hello John" as part of the system prompt. This is achieved by typing:

```
C:\> PROMPT Hello John ↵
```

This prompt remains valid until you switch off the PC. To change your prompt back to its original state, type:

```
C:\> PROMPT ↵
```

Setting the Date and Time

Just like setting the date and time in any modern electronic appliance, like a fax, video player and even a microwave, you can set the correct date and time on your PC. To change the date on your system, type:

```
C:\> date ↵
```

The system will display the message:

```
Current date is day mm-dd-yy
Enter new date (mm-dd-yy):_
```

To reset the date to 12th February 1993, for example, type:

```
02-12-93↵
```

If you don't want to change the date just press

```
↵
```

You could change the date by just typing today's date after the date command:

```
C:\> date 07-30-93 ↵
```

Similarly to set the system time, you can just type:

```
C:\> time ↵
```

The system will display:

```
Current time is 10:24:57.85a
Enter new time:_
```

To set the time to 1.35 p.m. type:

```
13:35↵
```

The proper time format is:

TIME hh:mm:ss:cc

where seconds (ss) and hundredths of seconds (cc) are optional. Note that the computer has a 24-hour clock.

If you want to change the time without seeing the current time, just type:

```
C:\> time 13.35 ↵
```

Selecting Disk Drives

Each disk drive on your PC is given its own identity. Your hard disk drive, if you have one, is labelled the 'C' drive. Your floppy disk drive is labelled 'A', and 'B' if you have a second one.

When you switch on your PC, the system accesses Drive A for *system files*. If there is no disk in this drive, it accesses the hard disk drive (Drive C), if the PC has one. If Drive A has any other disk, the system will display the message:

```
Non-system disk or disk error
Replace and press any key when ready
```

If you don't have a hard disk, then before you start your PC, make sure that your system disk is in Drive A.

The *system files* will be loaded in your *RAM* automatically (see Chapter 1). When this procedure is completed, your computer is ready for you and it will display the appropriate disk drive letter, prompt, and the cursor:

```
C:\>_
```

or `A:\>_`

You can easily change from accessing one disk drive to another. For example, to change from disk Drive C to A, type:

```
C:\>a: ↵
```

Now the prompt will change to:

```
A:\>
```

If you do not have a disk in Drive A, you will get the following message:

```
Not ready reading drive A
Abort, Retry, Fail?
```

To get out of Drive A, just type F for Fail.

Contents of your Disk

The next thing you may want to do is to see what is on your disk. To get a list of the contents type:

```
C:\>dir ↵
```

(dir is short for directory)

A list of all files in your C Drive will be displayed with the date and the time each file was created and the number of bytes used by each file. The total number of files on the disk and the number of bytes free on the disk will also be displayed:

```
Volume in drive C has no label
 Volume Serial Number is 337A-1501
 Directory of C:\COMPSTEP
.             <DIR>      14/07/92   21:45
..            <DIR>      14/07/92   21:45
SAMPLE   DOC     253899 20/07/92   13:28
REPORT   DOC        833 23/09/92   10:37
        4 file(s)     254732 bytes
                    27414528 bytes free
```

You can print this list if you have a printer connected to your PC. Type:

```
C:\>dir >prn ↵
```

If you have a large number of files on your disk, use the following variations to the directory command to make it easier to see them all:

Use `C:\>dir /w ↵` (w for wide display)

This will display only the file names, in up to five columns.

Use `C:\>dir /p ↵` (p for page at a time)

This will list all the information in one column but the list will pause each time the screen is full. To continue with the list press any key.

Multi-level Directory Structure

If you are working with several types of software or if there is more than one person using your PC, the number of files on your disk can grow very quickly. To make it easy to locate particular files or programs, DOS provides us with the concept of *multi-level directory structure*. This allows you to group your files in a convenient way and keep the disk organised.

The first level in a multi-level directory is the root directory, which is created automatically when you *format* your disk. The *FORMAT* command is discussed a little later in this chapter, under Preparing your disk.

Within the root directory, you can create sub-directories. Within each sub-directory you can create files or more sub-directories.

All sub-directories in your directory list will be indicated by the term '(dir)' after its name.

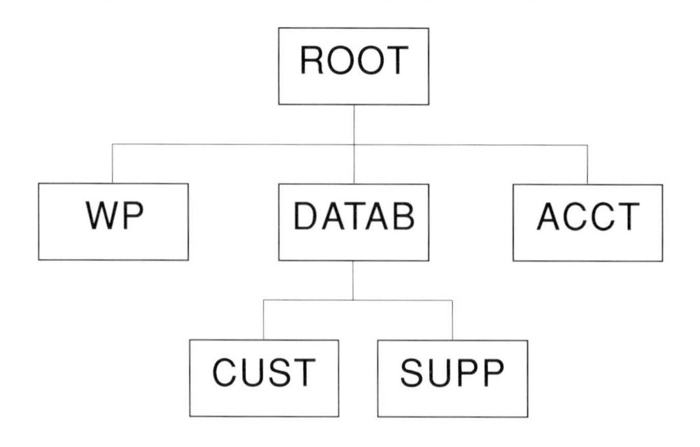

An example of a DOS directory tree

An important concept to learn about a multi-level directory is that of *pathnames*. A pathname is the precise route that DOS needs to know to find a file. For example, to find a file, called FINDME.TXT, stored in the directory, CUST (shown above), the pathname will be:

```
C:\DATAB\CUST\FINDME.TXT
```

Nowadays, most software comes with an automatic installation procedure, whereby it creates its own sub-directory and then copies its program files in this sub-directory. If you need to make your own sub-directories use the *MAKE DIRECTORY* command.

Say you wanted to install your accounts software on your PC, create a sub-directory, as follows:

```
C:\> md ACCT   ↵
```

Note that 'md' stands for Make Directory. If you want to see what is in your ACCT sub-directory, type:

```
C:\> dir C:\ACCT   ↵
```

or you can change your current directory first and then view the list of files in ACCT:

```
C:\> cd ACCT   ↵
```

where, 'cd' stands for Change Directory. If the system prompt is set up to display your current directory, then you should have the following on your screen:

```
C:\ACCT>
```

At some later stage you may want to remove your accounts system from your PC. You can take out your ACCT directory from your hard disk by typing:

```
C:\> rd ACCT   ↵
```

'rd' stands for Remove Directory. This will only work if there are no files in the sub-directory. You must delete all files from your sub-directory before attempting to remove it from your disk. See 'Deleting files' later for details on deleting files.

File Names

To recognise different files on your disk, the first thing you need to understand is DOS conventions for naming files. A filename can only have up to 8 characters. Although it can have an extension of up to 3 characters, provided that there is a period between the file name and the file extension. Eg. compstep.txt

Some files have extensions such as ".EXE", ".COM" and ".BAK". These are special types of files. Normally, the extension is used to describe the *file type*. A file type with an extension of .EXE means that it is an executable file. If you typed the file name without this extension, a program will be executed. Most software you buy will have at least one file with this extension. A file name with .COM is a command file e.g. FORMAT.COM. Here if you type the file name and other relevant information, like *FORMAT A:,* the program to format disks will be run. Finally, .BAK is a backup file which is quite often created automatically by some software, just in case your main file is corrupted and you need to use a backup.

For any document files you create, use file extensions to categorise your file types so that you can later identify your files easily. For example: RPT for reports, FRM for forms and LTR for letters.

There are certain characters, such as space and asterisk, that you cannot use when naming your files.

Important Files

You should be aware of various important DOS files that will be on your *system disk* or the root directory. You can customise them for your own particular system and requirements. These are:

Config.sys

This file contains commands needed to set up, or configure your PC. When you start your computer, DOS accesses this file for information such as number of files it can have open and maximum number of disk drives you may access. You would use this file to specify tasks that you want your PC to do automatically every time you start your PC. E.g. to connect devices such as your mouse.

Autoexec.bat

After DOS has completed all the tasks specified in the config.sys file, it will search for the autoexec.bat file. Config.sys can only be used to specify certain tasks. Autoexec.bat is used to specify all other tasks you may want your PC to perform everytime you start your PC. These may include: automatic installation of certain software, such as a menu system; or specification of your personalised system prompt.

Other BAT Files

When you install your software you will notice that it will add files in your directory with the extension '.BAT'. These are batch processing files containing several DOS commands that you would need to type when using your software. These files are used to 'batch' a series of DOS commands so that you only need to issue one command - the name of the file without the '.BAT' extension - to get DOS to perform several tasks.

TXT and DOC Files

Document files created using a word processor are usually given a file extension of either '.TXT' or '.DOC'. These files usually contain just text.

Contents of your Files

If you wish to see the contents of any file in your directory, use the *TYPE* command. To see what is in your autoexec.bat file, for example, type:

```
C:\> type autoexec.bat    ↵
```

Note that if you use this command to see files created by an application software, your PC may just bleep at you and only display some strange unmeaningful characters.

These are control characters used by the application software. You should go into the particular software package to display this information.

If it is a valid text file that you want to display, you may have more than one screenful of data in this file. The whole file will be displayed, but most of it will scroll out of sight before you have a chance to read it. You can control the scrolling of the screen display by using the following key combination to stop scrolling:

`Ctrl` and `S`   pressed simultaneously

To continue scrolling, press these keys again.

Preparing your Disks

Before you can use your hard disk and floppy disks for storing data, or programs, you need to prepare them for use. This is done by the *FORMAT* command. Formatting will structure your disk as shown below:

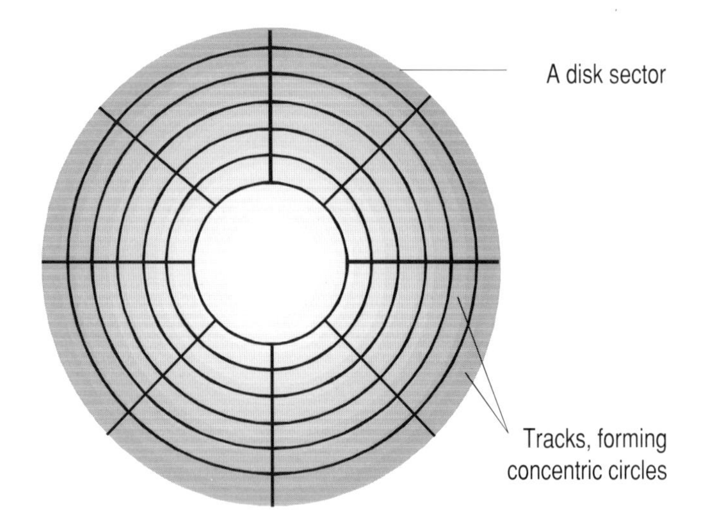

Format makes the disk look like a dart board

The number of tracks and sectors on a disk determines its storage capacity. The format command will automatically allocate the right number of these, depending on the storage capacity of your disk and the type of disk drive you have.

If you do not have a hard disk and you want to format a floppy disk, insert your system disk in Drive A and insert the disk to be formatted in Drive B. Then type:

```
A:\> format b: ↵
```

If you have a hard disk, to prepare it for use initially, type:

```
C:\> format c: ↵
```

To prepare a floppy disk, insert an unformatted disk in Drive A, and type:

```
C:\> format a: ↵
```

Note that you will only need to format your disk once before you copy any files on it. **The formatting procedure deletes any existing files on the disk.** So, always be careful when using this command.

If you accidently type 'c:' instead of 'a:' in the last command, you will format the hard disk, although the system will give you a warning which is something like:

```
WARNING, ALL DATA ON NON-REMOVABLE DISK
DRIVE C: WILL BE LOST!
Proceed with Format (Y/N)?
```

If you did not read the warning properly and typed 'Y' the consequence can be a disaster. You could loose many months of work that you have done and stored on the hard disk. When you buy a new PC, most manufacturers now provide the hard disk already formatted, so you should never need to do it yourself.

Other than the warning above, DOS unfortunately does not provide any protection against you wiping clean the hard disk. However, if you want to avoid formatting a floppy disk which contains important data or software, you should write-protect it.

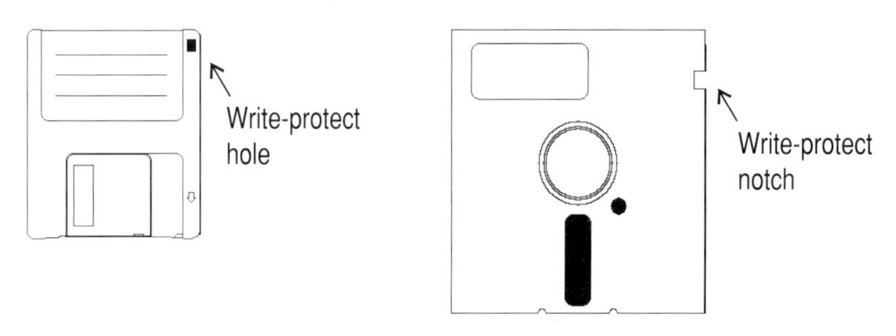

Write-protect areas on 3½ " and 5¼ " disks

If you write-protect a floppy disk, it will not accidently get formatted. Nor will you be able to write anything to the disk or delete files from it. To write-protect a 5¼" disk, stick a tab over the notch on the top righ-hand corner of the disk. When you buy 5¼" disks, several of these tabs are included in the box. To write-protect a 3½" disk, push up a little plastic slider with a ball-point nib so that a small hole is revealed.

If however, you did want to format a floppy disk and you had entered the *FORMAT* command, you will get the following message:

```
Insert new diskette for drive A
and press ENTER when ready...
```

Follow this instruction and when the disk is formatted you will get the confirmation:

```
Format complete
```

The system will then ask you for a volume label. Label your disk so that you can identify the data on it. This may be something like 'accounts' or 'wpfiles'. A label name can have up to eleven characters.

When your PC has completed labelling the disk, you will get details such as the total disk space available and a prompt to format another disk if you want to.

Copying Files

When you become an active PC user you will need to take copies of your files quite regularly. DOS allows you to copy files at several levels: at file level (this includes copying several files with some identical characters in the filenames), sub-directory level and disk level.

The basic DOS command for copying files is the *COPY* command. The general format is:

```
C:\> copy from  to
```

To copy individual files: For example - to copy one file, compstep.rpt, from your C Drive to a floppy disk in your A Drive, type:

```
C:\> copy c:\compstep.rpt a:↵
```

This will copy the file and give it the same name. The computer will also give the message:

```
1 File(s) copied
```

If you want to give the file a different name, say, compstep.cpy, type:

```
C:\> copy c:\compstep.rpt a:\compstep.cpy
```

If the file is in your word-processor sub-directory, called ‘wp’, you need to specify this:

```
C:\> copy c:\wp\compstep.rpt a:\compstep.cpy
```

If you want to copy it within a sub-directory, called ‘wpbackup’, and keep the same filename, type:

```
C:\> copy c:\wp\compstep.rpt a:\wpbackup
```

To copy several files with some identical characters in their filenames, you need to be aware of the *wild card* concept. To enable us to manipulate several files at the same time, DOS uses this concept, as in a game of playing cards. DOS wildcard characters are the question mark (?) and the asterisk (*), where the question mark replaces one character and the asterisk replaces a string of characters.

You can use wildcards to get your PC to select several files, disregarding the character replaced by a question mark, or the string of characters replaced by an asterisk.

For example, if you want to copy the following files in your sub-directory, wp, to a floppy:

compstep.rpt
sales.rpt
purchases.rpt
computer.rpt

You can use the command:

```
C:\> copy c:\wp\*.rpt a:   ↵
```

If you want to just copy compstep.rpt and computer.rpt, use:

```
C:\> copy c:\wp\comp????.rpt a:   ↵
```

When your PC has completed copying the files specified, it will display the message:

```
compstep.rpt
computer.rpt

                    2 File(s) copied
```

You can use the wildcard concept to copy all files within a directory or a sub-directory:

```
C:\> copy c:\*.* a:   ↵
```

or

```
C:\> copy c:\wp\*.* a:   ↵
```

You can issue the copy command from your sub-directory:

```
C:\> cd wp   ↵
```

```
C:\wp> copy *.*  a:    ↵
```

You can use the *COPY* command to copy all files from a root directory, as shown. Alternatively, if you have two floppy disk drives, you can use the *DISKCOPY* command to copy all files from one floppy disk to another and *DISKCOMP* to then compare the contents of the disks.

The general format of these commands are:

```
diskcopy source-drive target-drive

diskcomp source-drive target-drive
```

To copy all files from one floppy to another, insert your original disk in Drive A and a blank formatted disk in Drive B and type:

```
C:\> diskcopy a: b:
```

When copying is completed you will get the message:

```
copied successfully
```

Then, to compare the two disks, type:

```
C:\> diskcomp a: b:
```

If both disks are identical, you will get the message:

```
Compared OK
```

Deleting Files

To delete files from your disk you simply use the *DELETE* command:

```
C:\> del filename
```

The 'del' is an abbreviation for 'delete'. You can also use 'erase filename' to delete files. If you want to delete the file report.cpy in a sub-directory, wpbackup, on a floppy disk, insert the disk in drive A and type:

```
C:\> del a:\wpbackup\report.cpy ↵
```

The system will return the message:

```
1 file deleted
```

You can use wild cards to delete more than one file at a time, as you would when copying files.

A word of warning: If you fail to specify the disk drive when issuing a DOS command, it is assumed that you mean the current drive. So if you wanted to delete all files in your floppy in Drive A and you typed:

```
C:\> del *.* ↵
```

instead of

```
C:\> del a:*.* ↵
```

You will lose everything on your hard disk.

When issuing the *DELETE* command, try to get into the habit of working from the drive and sub-directory holding the files. For example, to delete everything from your sub-directory, wpbackup, on a floppy:

Make Drive A your current drive:

```
C:\> a: ↵
```

Make wpbackup your current sub-directory:

```
A:\> cd wpbackup  ↵
```

Then issue the *DELETE* command:

```
A:\wpbackup> del *.*  ↵
```

Your computer will return with the system prompt when it has deleted all the files.

Printing Files

Normally, to print data files, you should use the print facility in your software package. This will enable you to print the document in its proper format. However, if you want to print something else, like the documentation of a shareware program held on disk or the autoexec.bat file, use an extension of the *COPY* command:

```
C:\> copy autoexec.bat prn ↵
```

If you want to print a short file displayed on your screen, then press the 'Print Screen' key on your keyboard. This will print an exact image of your screen. You can even use this key to print a graphical screen from within a software package, provided your printer is able to print graphics.

Renaming Files

DOS allows you to change names of your files. This function is very useful when you have created a document and given it an appropriate filename. But after few meetings with your colleagues, the scope of the document changes.

The general format of the command is:

```
rename oldfilename newfilename
```

These examples will give you an idea of how this command is used:

To change filename compstep.rpt to company.rpt, type:

```
C:\> ren compstep.rpt company.rpt ↵
```

To change file extensions of all files from rpt to doc, type:

```
C:\> ren *.rpt *.doc ↵
```

To change a file called compstep.cpy on a floppy to compstep.rpt, insert the correct disk in Drive A and type:

```
C:\> ren a:\compstep.cpy comstep.rpt
```

Protecting your Data

If you have gone to the extent of buying a computer to process your data then your data must be quite important to you. You will want to do your utmost to avoid losing it. Data is stored on the hard disk or on floppies. The most common cause of data loss is: human error (I'm afraid). As you have seen, a slight mistake in typing your DOS command can wipe off your data. Next comes data lost because of hardware failure or a software problem. If your computer suddenly packs up when you are in the middle of your work then the files in your current application may get *corrupted*. Or, a *bug* in your software may do strange things to your data. The last and often overlooked case is when the data storage media itself is damaged or lost by theft or natural disasters such as fire or flood.

To avoid losing all the data from the day you started to use your system, you should take copies of your data on a regular basis, and keep the copies protected in a separate place from where your computer is.

DOS provides the *BACKUP* and *RESTORE* commands specifically for this purpose. The *BACKUP* command, just like the *COPY* command, copies files from one disk to another. But the *BACKUP* command checks the disk space on floppies and splits the files as necessary to use the space efficiently. This means that you can take backups of large files from your hard disk to several floppies without you needing to worry about noting down which files are held on which disk.

Because of this extra function controlled by the *BACKUP* command you must use the *RESTORE* command to recover, or recopy your files back to your original disk. You cannot use the *COPY* command to recopy files that have been 'backed-up'. Also, you must keep the disks with back-up data in the sequence they were used.

Although these commands may be used to backup and restore files from one floppy disk to another, they are really designed to handle large amounts of data usually held on the hard disk.

To backup your data you will need to format one or more floppy disks, depending on how much data you are backing up. If you are backing up just a few small files, then one floppy should be enough. If, however, you are backing up the whole of your 40 Mb hard disk, then you may need up to 60 3½" floppies.

Insert one formatted floppy disk in your A Drive:

To backup all files on your hard disk, type:

```
C:\> backup c:*.* a:   ↵
```

To backup your ACCOUNTS sub-directory, type:

```
C:\> backup c:\accounts\*.* a:   ↵
```

To backup one file, compstep.rpt, in your ACCOUNTS sub-directory, type:

```
C:\> backup c:\accounts\compstep.rpt a:
```

Your computer will prompt you to insert a blank formatted disk as each disk is filled up. Label these disks in a logical sequence, such as 1,2,3.... or A,B,C.... so that you can maintain the sequence if you ever need to recover the data.

To restore all files on your hard disk, type:

```
C:\> restore a: c:*.* ↵
```

To restore your ACCOUNTS sub-directory, type:

```
C:\> restore a: c:\accounts\*.* ↵
```

To restore one file, compstep.rpt, in your ACCOUNTS sub-directory, type:

```
C:\> restore a: c:\accounts\compstep.rpt
```

When you type this command, you will be prompted to insert the correct disk in Drive A. Insert the first disk in the sequence and press the 'Enter' key.

The restore program will continue to prompt you to insert the next disk, until the last disk is processed.

Re-booting your System

This does not mean that you kick your PC with your boots. Re-booting your system means to restart DOS without switching your computer off. The system will release anything that is in its *memory*, so make sure you have saved any work you need before you re-boot. To re-boot:

Press the RESET button on your PC

If you don't have a RESET button, then press the following keys simultaneously:

Ctrl Alt Del

Time Saving Tips

DOS uses the function keys (F1,F2,..) on your keyboard to save you time when issuing DOS commands. Two of the most useful keys are F1 and F3. You can use these keys to correct typing errors or to repeat commands:

F3 - to repeat the previous command

F1 - to repeat one character from the previous command

DOS Shell

DOS Shell is an added facility to your basic MS-DOS software. It provides you with a menu to perform the same functions you have learned, without the need to type DOS commands. You can issue commands with a click of a mouse instead of typing characters in the DOS command line. More importantly, instead of the normal prompt with a blinking cursor displayed, DOS Shell prompts you with various options and commands so that you do not need to look up or memorise the actual commands.

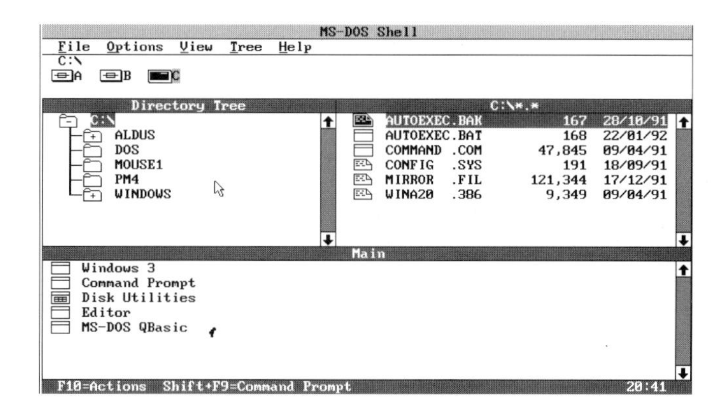

The MS-DOS Shell available with version 5.0

In the early days, you had to buy the DOS Shell as a separate software utility. In 1988 Microsoft released MS-DOS Version 4, which included its own DOS Shell, called MS-DOS Shell. This shell is also available with newer versions of MS-DOS, including MS-DOS 5.0.

If you do not have the time to learn commands or if you cannot remember them, then DOS Shell is a convenient way of becoming productive quickly.

To learn DOS further, read Computer Step's book on DOS for beginners.

Windows

Windows has revolutionised the way you use your PC. Most software companies have either developed or are developing windows version of their products. There is no doubt that this environment is of great importance to the PC. It is developed by the same company that has given us DOS - Microsoft.

Microsoft Windows is an easy-to-use Graphical User Interface (referred to as GUI - pronounced 'gooey') which sits on top of DOS. What this means is that it uses pictures, called *'icons'* to represent programs and files. You can select and run your applications by simply clicking twice on a particular icon (representing a software package) with a mouse. You can also perform many of the functions provided by DOS within this environment.

Windows does not replace DOS. Your PC still needs DOS to interact with Windows. It is just a very friendly piece of software between you and DOS. If you invest in Windows you can save yourself the trouble of learning many of the common DOS commands.

If you were reading the computer press during the 1990's when Windows 3 was released, you wouldn't have missed all the hype about this product. The industry pundits were predicting how Windows will boost sales of PCs and how DOS with Windows will be the main PC operating system/user interface for the future. As far as product popularity goes, over a million copies were sold in the first three months of the release!

The main reason for such excitement was that with GUI, it's a lot easier to use a PC and as a result you become more productive sooner. For the beginner, the learning curve is reduced dramatically. Icons give clues to what programs you want to start or commands you want to issue. Hence, you don't need to spend time learning DOS commands.

The other factor that makes Windows so attractive is that software designed to run with it, has a standard, consistent 'look and feel'. You have the same menu structure on the first screen of an application. For example, if you have Files as an option, you can expect to find functions like Save and Exit under this option. Non-windows software applications have different ways of performing basic functions, so you need to spend time to find out the basic commands, each time you use a new application.

Other major benefits that Windows offers are *multitasking* and *dynamic data exchange (DDE)*. Although at this stage you probably would not find much use for these facilities you might as well be aware of what's on offer. Multitasking means performing several tasks simultaneously. Windows offers users the facility of running several programs at the same time. If you have to print a large document that takes quite a while to print, for instance, you can issue the print command from your word-processor to start the print job, leave it printing and open another *window* to start work on your spreadsheet.

DDE allows you to set up 'hot-links' between common data in different software on your system. What this means in practice is that if you had the same data in more than one software, you can set up a link so that each time you change your data in one application, the data on the other software will be updated automatically. For example, if you had a table in your spreadsheet, which is also a part of your document in your word processor, you can link the two so that everytime you change your table in the spreadsheet, your document in the word processor will be updated automatically.

Although Windows is quite inexpensive for what it offers, its system requirements can add a lot to your budget. To run Windows you need a PC with at least 80286 microprocessor, 2Mb RAM, 20 Mb hard disk and an EGA screen. This is the minimum you will need. If your budget allows, go for the ideal set up: 80386 or higher processor, 4Mb RAM, 50 Mb hard disk and a VGA screen. With this you will have enough capacity to run most of the major applications under Windows and have a higher resolution display.

If you install Windows, you'll need to buy software with versions that are specifically developed for it. These versions should not cost you any more than the non-Windows versions. If you have already purchased some non-Windows versions, don't worry. You can still run them from Windows, but they will look and run as they normally do, without the superior interface that Windows applications offer.

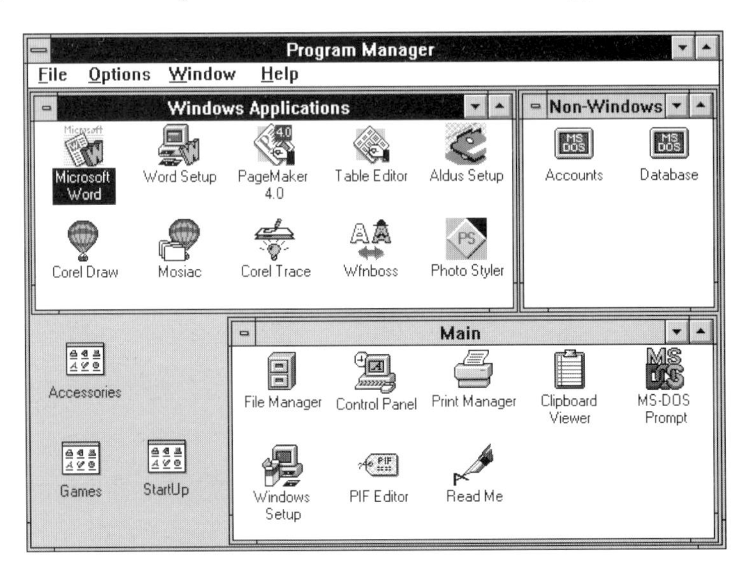

Windows presents applications graphically

For a quick training course in using Windows, see my book entitled *Windows in Easy Steps.*

Let your PCs do the talking

Once you realise the full capabilities of a PC, you will want to use it for many more applications. For example, how about making your PC talk to other computers? The official term used for this is *computer communications*. This is one of the most interesting areas within the world of computers. More and more of us will be using computer communications this decade. It can allow instant and economical transfer of data from say, Sydney (Australia) to London; or any other place in the world. People will be able to work from home much more easily, and tasks like shopping and banking may be done, on a mass scale, without going out. As an example, the Bank of Scotland already provides home banking by using computer communications technology. This type of technology is widely used today for many different purposes. Unfortunately, there is a lot of jargon used. This chapter aims to explain some of the "buzz" words, as well as the basic concepts.

In very basic terms, computer communication is two computers "talking" to one another. This is rather like two people talking to each other over the telephone. In fact, the telephone line is also used for computers, and just like voice communication, computer communication is instantaneous. To a computer user sitting in front of a screen receiving data, there is no difference if the sending computer is situated in the next room or many thousands of miles away.

Computer communication usually involves sending information from one PC to another over large distances via a telephone line. This is not to be confused with *Networking*, which is linking several PCs in a room or an office block with computer cables or wires.

To communicate using your PC, you need:

- A Modem
- A Telephone line
- A Communication program

Computer Signal

A computer can only really differentiate between high voltage and low voltage. After all, it is merely an electronic device. However, for it to be of any use to us, we need the computer to identify letters, numbers and special characters (like %, *). This is achieved by representing high voltage, typically 5 volts, as '1' and low voltage, which is zero volts, as '0'. And then, by using a series of '1's and '0's, all the characters on your keyboard are defined inside a PC. This method of representation is called a *Binary system*.

For example, the number '1' is represented by 00000001, number '2' by 00000010, the letter 'A' by 01000001, and so on. Each '0' or a '1' is called a *bit* (short for BInary digiT). A group of 8 bits represents a character or a value and it is called a *byte*.

Since everything inside a computer is represented by a string of '1's and '0's, the computer signal, or output that is generated by a computer, is a square wave:

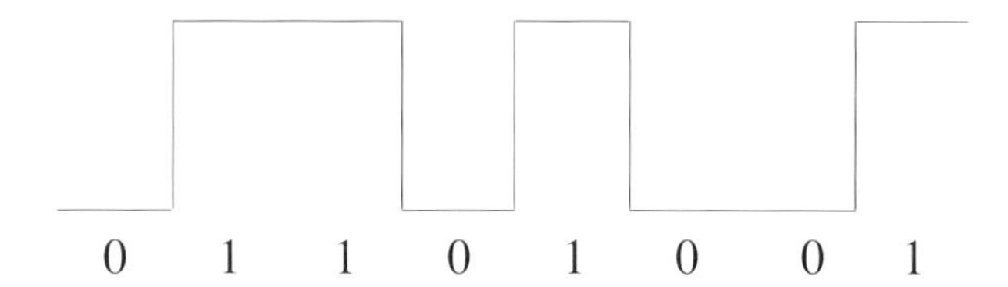

This is in sharp contrast to the type of wave we generate when we speak on the telephone. The human voice will generate a range of frequencies and thus produces a sine wave as shown below.

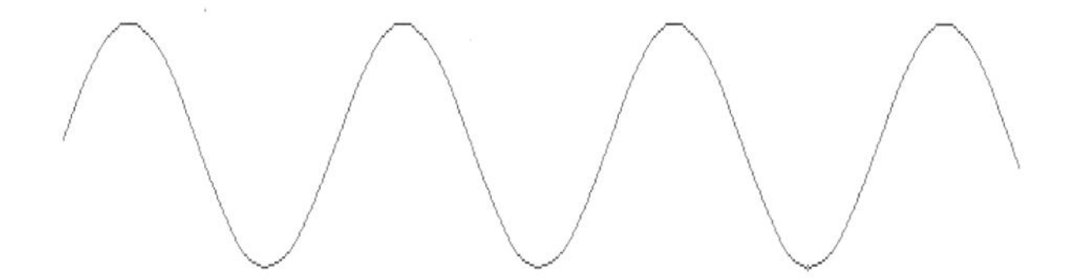

What is a Modem?

A modem converts computer generated output (a square wave) into frequencies that can be transmitted on a telephone line (a sine wave). This is necessary because the telephone line is not designed ideally to carry computer-generated signals. The receiving computer at the other end also requires a modem to convert back the telephone signals into computer ones. Hence, the name modem is derived from MOdulator-DEModulator.

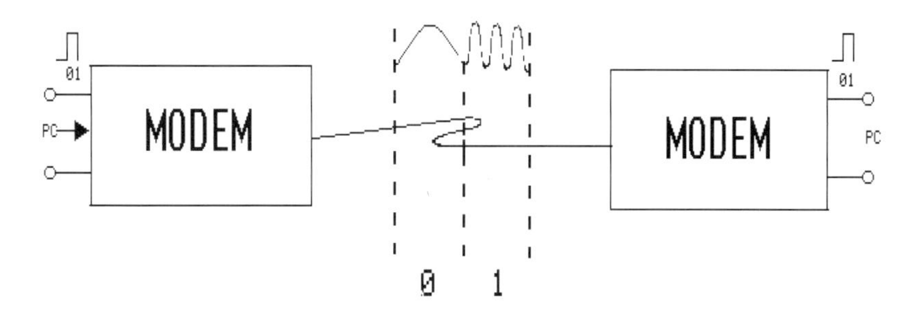

How a Modem translates between computer and telephone signals

Modems can either be available as a 'box', which you connect to the serial port (one of the sockets on the back of a PC) and the telephone line (called an external modem), or a card that you plug inside your computer (internal modem).

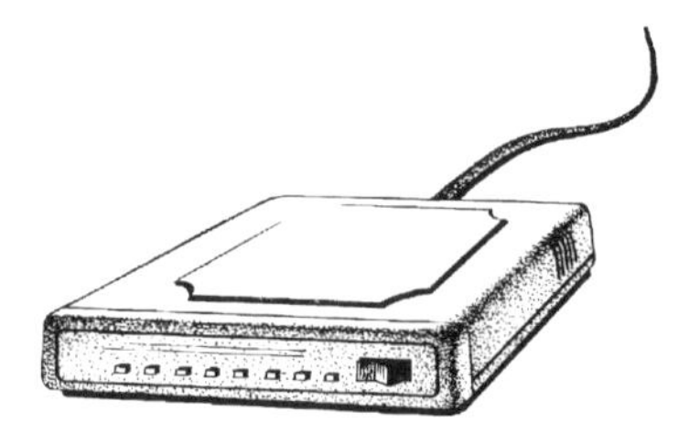

An External Modem

Speed of Transmission

The speed of data transmission depends directly on the type of modem you use. The reason for this is that the receiving modem must sample the frequency for a certain period of time to determine whether it is receiving a '0' or a '1'. This sampling time determines the transmission speed. Modems that only require a short sampling time and therefore offer faster transmission speeds are usually much more expensive. Transmission speeds are measured in *baud*, which is roughly equivalent to *bits per second*. Typical transmission speeds are 1200, 2400, 4800, 9600, 19200 baud.

Obviously, the faster the transmission speed the cheaper it is going to be in terms of telephone line charges, but the initial modem cost is going to be higher.

Ways of Transmitting

There are three different ways of transmitting information:

Simplex

This method of transmission is rarely used in computer applications. It is the simplest form of transmission, which is permanently in one direction.

Half Duplex

Here the transmission is in one direction at a given time. This is probably the most common way of communicating; not only via computers but for human communications too - unless you are one of those who talk when someone else is talking! The direction of transmission can be altered after a small delay. This delay is called the turnaround time.

A B

Duplex

In this case, the line is transmitting in both directions at the same time.

A B

Protocols

The term 'protocol' is often used in diplomatic circles. It is usually a document setting out the terms of a treaty or similar, which needs to be formally agreed and signed. Communication protocols, or 'handshaking' procedures, are also rules that are agreed beforehand. The transfer of data or information across the line usually requires quite a complex set of rules to ensure efficient and accurate transfer. They must cater for all possible contingencies, including errors in transmission and the failure of the line itself.

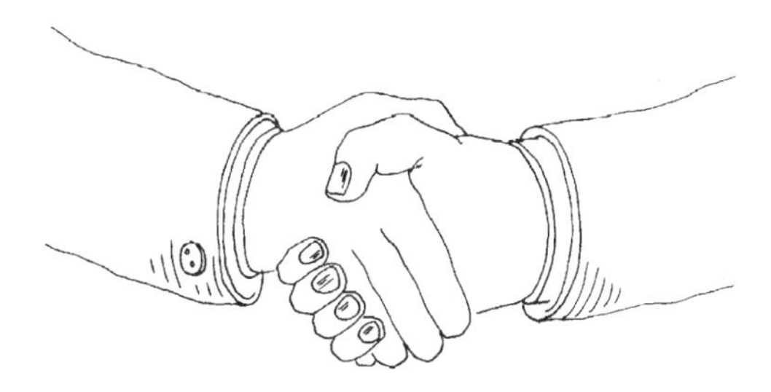

These handshaking procedures will usually be built into the communication software that is being used.

Error Checking

Every transmission is subject to potential errors. Errors may occur because of a faulty cable, poor switching, static electricity, and so on. These errors will create a burst of 'noise' in the line, which will tend to destroy or alter any data message being sent. Checks are therefore required to detect that an error has occurred. And if so, the receiving computer needs to ask the sending computer to re-send the message.

Parity

This is a very simple way of checking for errors. You can either operate on an *Odd* parity or an *Even* parity. Basically, instead of using 8-bits to represent a character, 7-bits are used - an extra bit is added to the end to represent the parity bit. If you are using an even parity and the number of '1's in your character is an odd number, than the extra parity bit added will be a '1' to make the whole byte an even number of bits. If however, the number of bits is even, than the parity bit will be a '0' to maintain an even number of bits. An odd parity system will work in a similar way, but maintaining an odd number of bits.

1 1 0 0 0 0 1 **1** *bit added for even parity*

The receiving computer will check that all characters conform to either odd or even parity. If they don't, then something has gone wrong and some of the data may need to be re-transmitted.

Check Sum

In general, communication errors will affect a number of bits rather than one individual bit. Consequently, error checks need to be more complex than the simple parity check. Most communication software today uses a check sum method of error checking.

The way this works is that a calculation is performed on the value of each character being sent in a block, and a total is derived, which is completely dependent on the particular data being sent. This total is the *check sum* and is tagged at the end of the block of data being transmitted. The receiving computer will extract the data bytes from the block and apply the same check sum formula. It will compare its result with that it received. If it matches then the transmission was error-free. If not, then, that block of data needs to be re-transmitted with the same checks being performed again.

Transmission packet

Echo Check

This is probably the most commonly used method of error checking. It is performed by us every time we use a PC. It is best illustrated with a diagram:

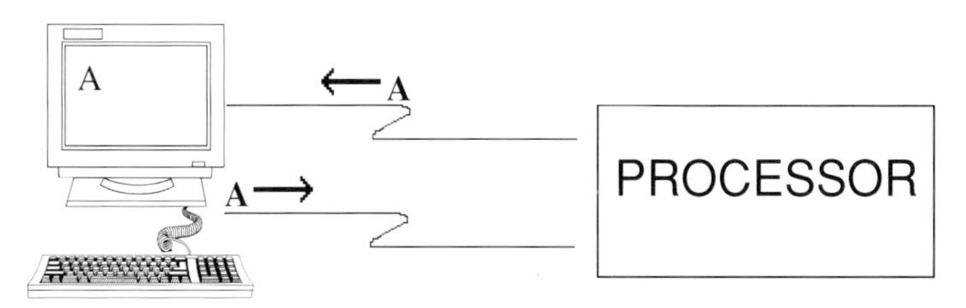

The transmission of the letter 'A'

Although a telephone line is not used here you are still transmitting data from your keyboard to the memory of your computer. The data is also echoed to the monitor so that you can check for yourselves that you are entering the correct information.

Asynchronous Transmission

Most of the communication today is asynchronous. The reason for this is that it is the simpler and the cheaper method. With asynchronous transmission, each character is transmitted separately. There is a start bit sent before each byte to 'wake up' the receiving computer. Then, there are 7 or 8 bits sent to represent the actual data byte. At the end, a stop bit, or sometimes two, will indicate end of a byte of information.

The disadvantage of asynchronous transmission is that the line is fully connected during the 'think' time of the user. Also, the start and stop bits are an overhead.

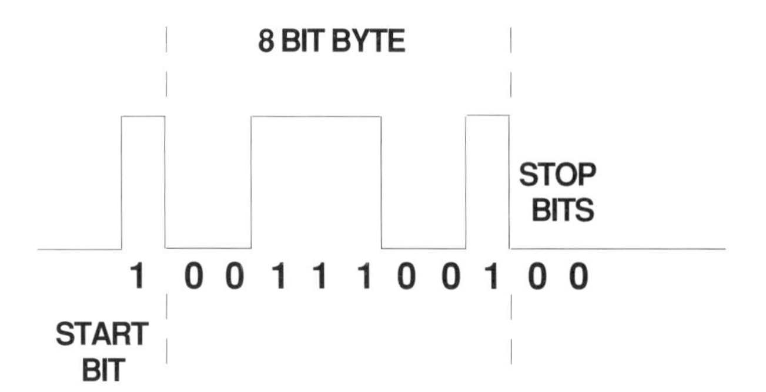

Synchronous Transmission

Synchronous transmission transmits information at a regular rate. Both the sending and receiving computers are synchronised for the duration of the message.

CONTROL INFO								CHECK SUM
			MESSAGE BYTES					

What is a BBS?

A bulletin board system (abbreviated BBS) is a central bank of information that users call to exchange ideas, tips and public domain software via their modems.

You can send information to a BBS so that anyone who calls will have access, or alternatively, you can address your message to particular individuals. The latter, is termed 'Electronic mail'.

Most BBSs are free and run by hobbyists. They are, however, not very up-to-date in the information they provide and you may find them to be engaged a lot of the time.

Popular commercial BBSs include:

CompuServe

This is a US-based system, but has many dial-in points in the UK and other countries. It is probably the world's largest system. It has information on various specialist subjects. You can send messages to other members anywhere in the world and obtain technical help from many hardware and software vendors.

Prestel

This is run by British Telecom. It has over 300,000 screens of information. This includes news, sports, travel, finance, and microcomputing.

Blaise

This database contains all books ever held at the British Library since 1950.

Jordans and Kompass

Provides useful information on many UK companies.

The Last Word

By reading this book you have progressed a great deal; from knowing very little about computers to becoming computer literate. You are now ready to venture even further into the PC world.

To buy your PC system, you will need to compare specific brands of hardware and software. This book has prepared you to understand the literature on these products, so that you can make a fair comparison.

This book will also help you to get started with using your PC. The DOS commands covered in Chapter 4 will enable you to command your PC to do various tasks.

Once you are beyond this stage, there are several ways to progress further.

Books & Videos

There are thousands of different books that fall under the subject of computers. Most of these titles are on specific products such as *WordPerfect* or *DBase*. Although these software products come with basic user manuals, some books in the market are more readable than the manuals.

Most of the specialised computer books are quite expensive - it would be wise to browse through a title in the bookstore before buying it.

Educational videos on general computer principles and on more specialised topics are also now available. These are sometimes as much as four times more expensive than the usual movie videos. These videos are really produced and priced to be used by businesses to train a number of staff rather than for a private individual. Computer videos are not sold through high-street stores but usually by mail directly by the publishers. Some computer dealers and leading computer booksellers also supply them.

Computer Based Training

Computer based training, or CBT for short, is a term used to describe training packages that force you to use your PC to do the course. You interact with your PC to learn about the product and to do the exercises included in the course. The basic aim of CBT is to get the student to learn by practical experience. The good thing about using CBT is that you can progress at your own pace and nobody has to know how you are doing.

The main drawback of CBT is that it is a dearer way of learning than learning from books. CBT is, however, more effective and an interesting way of learning. It has become quite popular in businesses where a licence can be purchased from vendors to train a large number of staff.

Classroom Courses

Classroom courses are offered by technical colleges, polytechnics and some universities. You can attend on full or part time basis, or take evening classes. The range of courses offered vary from basic computing to using leading software packages like *Lotus 1-2-3*. The prices vary from college to college. They usually run during the school terms and throughout the summer period. Check with your local colleges on exact times and prices.

Classroom courses are also offered by private companies. These companies specialise in computer training. Again, their courses are aimed at businesses more than private individuals - indirectly, this means that they are expensive. Having said that, the quality of instructors used by these companies is high. To satisfy the business clients, these companies have to offer high standards.

User Groups

Anyone who uses a computer is called a *computer user*, or simply a *user*. A user group is formed when a pool of people using the same product or service keep in contact with each other to share their ideas and experiences. User groups are formed to help and offer advice to the members with their computer or with using the software. Some of these are free to join but most of them charge a nominal fee.

Members of user groups keep in touch by regular meetings, newsletters, telephone helplines, and even by bulletin boards.

Most of these user groups are independent from product vendors. However, they may maintain a close relationship. By joining user groups you can learn how to make the most of your computer or software. You can usually find answers to any problems you may be having with the product. You can even raise issues that bother you or make suggestions to the vendors on improving the product. Also, you usually get to know about any upgrades or any other changes earlier than you would otherwise.

Other ways to learn more about PCs are those already discussed in *Chapter 3, Let's Go Shopping*. Read computer magazines, especially the news sections and product reviews. Visit computer exhibitions now and then to keep up with changes in the industry and to see any new products being launched.

APPENDIX

Jargon Buster

APPLICATION PROGRAMS

Programs that perform specific tasks relating directly to business functions such as accounting and wordprocessing. Examples include: Sage and WordPerfect.

ASCII (pronounced 'Asky')

Stands for American Standards Code for Information Interchange. It is an agreed standard that specifies which numbers will represent which characters. Computers can only work with numeric digits so each character on your keyboard has to be converted to a number for processing.

ASSEMBLER

A programming language that directly interacts with the processor - hence it is called a 'low-level' language. It is also very hard to use.

AUTOEXEC.BAT

A special batch file that is used to 'batch' together several DOS commands that are to be executed everytime the PC is started up. DOS looks for this file when the PC is started up and automatically follows the commands that are contained in it.

BACKUP

A DOS command or a procedure to create an extra copy of program or data. It is usual to hold this spare (backup) copy on a different storage medium from the original. The backup copy can be used should the original data be corrupted or lost.

BASIC

Stands for Beginners' All-purpose Symbolic Instruction Code. One of the easiest programming languages to learn and use. Hence, it falls under the category of a 'high-level' language. BASIC can be used on most PCs.

BAUD RATE

The speed at which data is transmitted between computer devices is measured in baud. The faster the rate of transmission the higher the baud rate. The word baud originates from Baudot, a French inventor.

BBS

Stands for Bulletin Board System. It is a computer based online database which can be accessed by PC users with modems. Useful for finding and exchanging information on common interests.

BINARY

A numbering system where a numeric digit can only be 0 or 1. So a Decimal 2 is 10 and 3 is 11 and so on. Computers count using the binary system.

BIOS

Stands for Basic Input Output System. BIOS is a piece of coding that is stored in the computer's ROM (read only memory). Its basic function is to control the interaction between the processor and other hardware such as disk drives, keyboard and monitor.

BIT

Derived from BInary digiT, the term bit is a binary number, 0 or 1. The computer internally can only recognise a 1 which represents an 'on' switch and a 0 which represents an 'off' switch electronically. Eight bits are grouped together to form a byte, to represent a character.

BOOT

To boot a computer means to start a computer. The process involves switching the computer on and having it load up the operating system such as DOS.

BPS

An abbreviation for bits per second. Used to measure the speed of data transmission from one device to another.

BUFFER

A temporary storage area within the system. A buffer holds data until the main device such as computer memory or printer is ready to process it.

BUS

An electronic circuit within the PC through which data passes to go from one component to another. e.g. from memory to the processor.

BYTE

A byte consists of eight bits and represents a character. Memory size and disk capacity are measured in number of bytes.

C

A powerful programming language which has become very popular in the PC world. It falls in between high-level languages such as BASIC and low-level languages such as assembler.

CAD/CAM

Stands for computer aided design and computer aided manufacturing. CAD software allows draughtsmen to use computers to replace their drawing boards and tools for technical drawings and plans. CAM relates to use of computers to control robotic tools for manufacturing.

CD-ROM

Acronym for compact disc read-only memory. Just another medium for read-only-memory. A CD allows storage of masses of data - it offers storage capacity of up to several hundred megabytes rather than the normal 4 or 8 megabytes. Used for storing large amounts of data that will never need to be changed.

CGA

Colour graphics adapter (for PC monitor). The first colour screen for the IBM PC and compatibles, but by today's standards, the screen resolution offered with CGA is considered poor.

CHARACTER
A letter, numeral or a symbol that is on your keyboard or displayed on your screen.

CHIP
Short for microchip. A thin rectangular silicon wafer on which electronic circuits are built. It is boxed in a black or grey casing with metal contacts.

CLIPART
A computer-generated picture or drawing you can purchase and use within your own DTP work.

CLONE
A computer that is not made by IBM but works in exactly the same way. It runs the same software as the original IBM, but it is quite often cheaper.

CMOS
Stands for complementary metal oxide semiconductor. Used to produce memory and microprocessor chips which need less voltage and can be powered by battery. CMOS chips are often used in laptops and other portables.

COMMS
Short for communications. The term is used to describe the process of transferring data from one computer to another via the use of modems and telephone lines. Not to be mixed up with networks, which involves connecting several computers (usually with cables) so that data may be shared.

CONFIG.SYS
A text file that DOS looks for when the system is started up. It holds information on the system set-up and configuration, such as how to communicate with various hardware.

CPU
An acronym for central processing unit, also referred to as microprocessor, or just processor. This is the component in a computer where all the work is done. It is the CPU that follows your commands and performs the specified tasks.

CURSOR
A flashing line or a square on your screen. When you type on your keyboard, the characters

will appear on your screen where the cursor is positioned. As you type, the cursor will advance automatically.

DATA

Information that is stored on disks or processed by programs. This may be name, address, amount and so on.

DATABASE

A collection of data stored in a orderly manner so that future retrieval for searching, sorting or printing is easily achieved. Also used to refer to software that provides facilities to do this. The proper name for this type of software is a database management system (DBMS).

DEFAULT

When there is more than one option or setting available, the computer will be programmed to select one, usually the most common one, as the default. If you do not specify any preference, the computer will take it that you wish to opt for the default setting or option and continue processing accordingly.

DEVICE DRIVER

A software program that will allow DOS to work with specific hardware such as a printer or a scanner. You should get this program on one or more floppy disks when you purchase your hardware.

DISK

A media used for permanent storage of computer based data and programs. Most disks have a form of magnetic coating on which data is recorded.

DISK CACHE

An area in computer's RAM (random access memory) which is used to hold a copy of frequently accessed data. It is quicker for the processor to access data from the memory rather than from the hard disk. Disk caching is a way of increasing processing speed by saving on this access time.

DISK CONTROLLER

A disk controller is a major component of a hard disk. It is a board that plugs into the motherboard. It controls the mechanism for accessing, reading and writing data to the hard disk.

DISK DRIVE

A disk drive is part of the system unit of a computer. It holds disks, reads data from disks and writes data on disks. A disk drive and a disk must be compatible in terms of physical size and capacity.

DOS

Short for Disk Operating System. DOS is an operating system for the IBM PC and compatibles that is loaded from disk.

DPI

An acronym for dots per inch. DPI is used to measure resolution of output from scanners and laser printers.

DR DOS

An abbreviation for Digital Research Disk Operating System. A competitor to Microsoft (MS) DOS. It offers extra features and it is completely compatible with MS-DOS - it will run the same programs and obey the same commands.

DTP

Short for Desktop Publishing and means using a computer to combine text and graphics on a page to produce magazines, newsletters, books etc. Replaces time-consuming traditional methods of manually cutting and pasting text/graphics. Also used to refer to software that provides facilities to achieve this such as Pagemaker, QuarkXpress, Ventura and PagePlus.

DUMP

A term used to refer to straightforward transfer of the contents of a file or a screen to a printer, for creating a hardcopy on paper.

EGA

Enhanced graphics adapter (for PC monitor). EGA is the next generation up from the CGA and provides improved resolution with more colours.

EISA (pronounced 'ee-sah')

An abbreviation for Extended Industry Standard Architecture. An alternative standard to MCA for PC's internal bus architecture. Formed by IBM's competitors, it was designed to be used for clones more powerful than the IBM AT.

E-MAIL

A system which allows sending and receiving of messages between users on linked computers. These computers may be linked by modems or networks.

EMULATION

A way of programming one computer to believe and behave as if it was another.

ESC KEY

The ESC (escape) is usually located on the top left-hand corner of your keyboard. Use it to return to the previous screen or mode.

EXPANDED/EXTENDED MEMORY

Different types of memory that can be added to the standard one megabyte memory that DOS can address. Expanded memory may be added to any PC but can only be accessed in blocks of 64K from a pool of memory. However, not all software is able to use expanded memory. Extended memory, on the other hand, is continuous memory that can be accessed and manipulated as required, but can only be installed on a PC with a 286 processor or higher.

EXPANSION CARD/SLOT

A circuit board that fits into an expansion slot on the motherboard inside the computer. Just as the name implies, it allows you to add extra features such as more memory or to connect a modem to the PC.

FILE

A collection of information held together under one entity. The information may be a program, customer data, a letter from a wordprocessor or a report from an accounting system.

FLOPPY DISK

A permanent form of storage medium that may be separated from the computer. There are two types available for the PC: 5.25" and 3.5". The latter is made with a stronger casing and has a higher storage capacity.

FONT

Means a particular type of typeface or a typestyle. E.g. Times Roman, Script. The proper reference to a font should also include the point size and style (e.g. italics, bold). However, quite often the word font is used instead of typeface.

FORMAT

A DOS command or a process of preparing disks for use. Formatting a disk involves dividing it up and allocating areas for data storage.

GIGABYTE

A gigabyte is equal to a billion bytes (to be exact 1,073,741,824 bytes), which is equal to one million kilobytes or a thousand megabytes.

GRAPHICS

Refers to pictures and drawings including lines, circles, squares or any other shapes produced using a computer. The term is also used to refer to software that allows you to draw and manipulate these objects.

GUI (pronounced 'gooey')

Short for graphical user interface. A friendly interface between the computer and the user; an alternative to a command-based interface like DOS. GUI usually provides option menus and icons (symbols) to make it easier to operate the computer. The most popular GUI product for the PC today is Windows by Microsoft.

HACKER

A person who is obsessed with computers. Often used to refer to a person who accesses and manipulates other people's computer without obtaining authority.

HARD DISK

A fixed disk usually installed inside the computer for the purpose of storage. It has far higher capacity and it is much more efficient to use than a floppy disk. For any serious work it is more practical to have a hard disk on your system.

HAYES-COMPATIBLE

Hayes is the company that manufactured Smartmodem, a modem for computer communications. The set of commands used by Hayes to instruct the modem are understood by most communications software. Other modems that use the same set of commands are classified as Hayes-compatible. This has also become the PC industry standard for modems.

HERCULES

Hercules Computers is the name of the company that first made monochrome graphics cards for the PC that could combine MDA (monochrome display adapter) text-only output with graphics. Cloned adapter cards that can achieve the same thing are referred to as Hercules compatible.

ICON

A visual picture or a symbol used to represent programs or documents in a GUI environment.

INTEGRATED SOFTWARE

An integrated software is a combination of applications packaged together and treated as one product. It usually consists of a wordprocessor, database, spreadsheet and some utility programs. An example of an integrated package is Works by Microsoft.

INTERLACED/NON-INTERLACED MONITORS

Super VGA monitors which offer very high resolution may be interlaced or non-interlaced. The difference between the two is in the way they update screens. Screens are updated by electron beams defining each dot on a screen in turn. This is usually done in one go (referred to as one scan). However, with high resolution Super VGA screens, the number of dots to be updated is extremely high making it expensive to update all the dots in one scan. To make screens more economical, interlaced screens are designed to update every other line in the first scan and the rest in the next scan. Unfortunately, this causes the screens to flicker. Non-interlaced screens update the whole screen in one scan and you will not have the problem of flickers. However, these are more expensive.

ISA (pronounced 'eye-sah')

An abbreviation for Industry Standards Architecture. The basic standard for the IBM AT machine and its clones.

K

Short for Kilobytes. One Kilobyte may be referred to as just 1K.

KEYBOARD

The main hardware device for entering data in a computer. A computer keyboard looks very much like a typewriter keyboard, but has extra keys for specific computer functions.

KILOBYTE

One thousand bytes. To be precise, 1,024 bytes (or 2 to the power of 10).

LAN
An acronym for local area network. LAN computers are linked together with cables and they are usually under one roof.

LCD
Stands for liquid crystal display. Most screens on portable PCs use LCD technology. A LCD screen uses liquid crystal shutters to display screen dots rather than electron beams used on desktop screens.

LOAD
Moving a program or data into the computer's memory, usually from a disk.

MACRO
One key or a command representing a sequence of keystrokes or commands. A number of frequently used keystrokes or commands may be defined and saved under one macro to avoid typing them again and again.

MATHS COPROCESSOR
A microchip that can process calculations, especially those involving fractions, at a much faster rate than the processor. It is fitted inside the computer. Software such as spreadsheets can perform much faster if the computer has a maths coprocessor.

MCA
An abbreviation for microchannel architecture. IBM's standard for PCs more powerful than the AT. Competes with EISA which was formed by companies manufacturing IBM clones.

MDA
Stands for monochrome display adapter (for PC screen). IBM's original PC screen used MDA. It can only generate text.

MEGABYTE
One million bytes. 1,048,576 bytes, to be precise. Also equal to one thousand Kilobytes.

MEMORY
A microchip that holds programs and data that is required by the processor. Unlike disks it only stores 'live' information.

MEMORY CACHE

An expensive type of memory which can be read and written to at a much faster rate than the ordinary memory. Used to hold 'live' information that is used frequently by the processor. The overall benefit of memory caching is that programs work at much faster speeds.

MEMORY RESIDENT PROGRAMS

Programs that are designed to stay in the memory next to DOS until called for. A lot of utility programs are designed to be memory resident. They sit in the memory until a special key is pressed to activate them. Also known as TSR - terminate and stay resident - programs.

MENU

A list of commands or options displayed on the screen, prompting the user to select one.

MICROPROCESSOR

Also known as a processor or a CPU (central processing unit). A microchip that actually performs all the specified tasks. It is installed on the motherboard inside the computer.

MIDI

Stands for musical instrument digital interface. An interface, including a port, for connecting musical instruments to the computer for composing music.

MODEM

Derived from MOdulator/DEModulator, it is a hardware device that is required for computers to be linked via telephone lines. A modem converts digital signals from computers to analogue signals required for transmission through the telephone system, and vice versa.

MONITOR

A synonym for computer screen, display or VDU. A monitor is the main device to see what you have typed and also for the computer to communicate to you.

MOTHERBOARD

Computer's main circuitry where the microprocessor and other chips are plugged.

MOUSE

An input device that is placed and moved around the desk to control cursor movements. It also has two buttons which may be used to select menu options and to manipulate text and objects on screen.

MS-DOS

Microsoft Disk Operating System. It is a disk operating system developed by Microsoft and has become the most popular operating system for the IBM PC clones. It is usually offered free when you buy a clone.

MULTITASKING

When a processor is performing more than one task at a time. Strictly speaking, the processor cannot really achieve this, but appears to be providing this service by executing a task (or a program) for a very short time and then switching to another task and so on. This technique is known as 'time-slicing' and it gives the impression that several programs are running simultaneously.

MULTIMEDIA

The art of using a computer for combining text, graphics, sound and video to present information.

NETWORK

A way of connecting computers so that they can share data, software programs as well as hardware such as printers.

ONLINE

Programs/information which can be accessed and made available from the computer immediately, without having to load them in from external storage media.

OPERATING SYSTEM

An operating system consists of a suite of programs that interface between the user, applications programs and the processor. It translates commands into machine language that the computer understands. It also controls the hardware and software.

OS/2

Stands for Operating System/2. An operating system for the PC and PS/2 intended by IBM to succeed DOS and Windows.

PARALLEL PORT

A port is a socket at the back of a computer where another device can be plugged into for exchanging information. A parallel port sends data a byte at a time and therefore it is faster than a serial port. It is usually used for connecting a printer and it is also known as a Centronics port.

PC

An acronym for personal computer. Used to refer to all microprocessors but since IBM introduced the IBM PC, it is used to mean the IBM PC and compatibles.

PC-DOS

Means IBM Personal Computer-Disk Operating System. The operating system supplied with the IBM PC. Although developed and licensed to IBM by Microsoft, Microsoft has its own version, MS-DOS which is used by most of the clones.

PERIPHERAL

Any device that is connected to the main computer, such as a printer or a modem.

PIXEL

A PICture ELement, or a dot on the computer screen. A pixel is the smallest element a screen can be divided into. The number of pixels a screen can generate determines the resolution - the higher the number of pixels the sharper the image.

PORTABLES

Computers that are designed to be carried around. Portables should be light and compact enough to be moved easily. Many of the models work on batteries so they can be used whilst on the move.

POSTSCRIPT

A language that instructs a laser printer what to print. It is referred to as a page description language because it defines the page to be printed rather than giving a set of instructions on what to print. Postscript laser printers are printers that can understand this language. For professional DTP work you will need a Postscript printer.

PRINTER

A hardware device that a computer needs to produce information on paper.

PROGRAM

A set of coded instructions for the computer to perform a specific task. There are two types of programs: system programs which include operating systems and application programs such as wordprocessors and spreadsheets.

PROMPT

When a computer is waiting for the user to enter a command or information, it will use a prompt to indicate this. E.g. C:\ is a prompt used by DOS.

PS/2

Stands for Personal System/2. In 1987 IBM introduced a series of personal computers under the PS/2 range. The underlying technology used for PS/2 models is very different from the IBM PC. Although the main operating system for PS/2 models is OS/2, DOS and Windows can still be used.

PUBLIC DOMAIN SOFTWARE

Software that the author has decided to distribute freely rather than selling it for a price. This means you should not pay for it nor sell it. You can copy it and use it as you like.

RAM

An acronym for random access memory. Storage memory inside the computer that may be written to and updated by the processor. RAM only holds 'live' data, which means that any updates must be saved on a hard or floppy disk before leaving the application or switching off the computer.

REAL TIME CLOCK

A battery powered clock inside the computer that maintains the time and date, even when the computer is switched off.

RESOLUTION

This determines how well defined text/graphics appear from a computer screen, printer or even from a scanner. The higher the number of dots (or pixels) representing output from these devices, the higher the resolution.

ROM

An acronym for read only memory. ROM is storage memory inside the computer that cannot be amended or erased by the processor. ROM is used to hold static information necessary for the computer such as the Basic Input Output System.

SCANNER

A hardware device that can read in visual images from paper and convert them into data files that can be manipulated by the computer.

SERIAL PORT

A port is a socket at the back of a computer where another device can be plugged into for exchanging information. Unlike the parallel port, a serial port transmits data one bit at a time. Used mainly for connecting a mouse or modem to a PC.

SHAREWARE PROGRAMS

Shareware is really a way of marketing computer software. Shareware programs are distributed freely like public domain software. However, authors request a nominal fee if you decide to continue using the software. When you register by paying your fee you will receive proper manuals and future updates.

SOFTWARE

Software consists of data and coded instructions (programs) for the computer. Software is held on hardware such as disks and memory.

SPREADSHEET

A spreadsheet is a method of performing elaborated calculations using rows and columns. A computer based spreadsheet allows you to assign value, text or formula to each element on the spreadsheet (known as a 'cell'). Once a formula is assigned to a cell, its value will be automatically calculated. A computer can also work out the effect of a change almost instantly. This makes it very useful for 'what if?...' analysis which would be very tedious and time-consuming to work out manually. Software packages that offer these facilities are also known as spreadsheets. Examples include Lotus 1-2-3 and Excel.

SURGE PROTECTOR

A peripheral device that protects the computer from power surges from the outlet where the PC is plugged in.

SUPER VGA

Super video graphics array is a display standard for PC monitors. Super VGA offers high resolution of 800 x 600 dots with 256 colours or 1,024 x 768 dots with 16 colours.

TERMINAL

A terminal is a display unit that is fed information from the main computer, called the host computer. A terminal may also have a keyboard and a printer connected to it.

TONER

Made of powder pigment, it is used by laser printers instead of ink to print an image.

TRACKER BALL

An input device used instead of a mouse. It looks like an up-side-down mouse, with the ball at the top. Instead of moving the whole device for cursor movements you just rotate the ball.

TSR PROGRAMS

TSR is short for terminate and stay resident. TSR programs are designed to stay in the memory for easy access, when required. They can be activated by simply pressing a key or a combination of keys. Sometimes also referred to as memory resident programs.

TYPEFACE

A style for a set of characters. Sometimes called fonts. Examples include: Times Roman, Helvetica and Bookman.

UNIX

A very powerful operating system for personal computers developed by AT & T Bell Laboratories. It is also widely used in minis and mainframe computers. Unix is designed for multitasking and multiuser environments.

VGA

An acronym for video graphics array. A standard set by IBM for colour monitors. Offers more colours and a sharper resolution than EGA.

VIRUS

A piece of software that is designed to corrupt information on the computer. It is programmed to run automatically, copy itself and spread to other linked computers via networks, modems or floppies.

WINCHESTER DISK

Another term for a hard disk. So called because many hard disks were invented in IBM's laboratories in Winchester, USA.

WINDOWS
A rectangular area on the computer screen which can be treated as an individual display that can hold information. Windows is also a GUI product by Microsoft which uses the concept of windows to allow running of more than one program simultaneously.

WORD PROCESSING
Using computers for producing letters and other documents. At its basic level, word processing supersedes the traditional typewriter, making it possible to edit text several times before finally printing it on paper. Today, most word processing packages offer a lot more than just the editing function: spell checking, macros, mail-merging and indexing are just a few examples.

WRITE PROTECT
A way of protecting data on your disks so that it does not get over-written or deleted.

WYSIWYG (pronounced 'wizzy-wig')
Stands for what you see is what you get. A facility offered by programs which can display text and graphics on your screen exactly as they will appear when printed on paper.

Index

D

E

F

L

M

N

O

P

Q

R

S

T

U

V

W